Cooking with Food Storage
Made Easy

Printed in China
First Printing: September 2009

14 13 12 11 10 09   10 9 8 7 6 5 4 3 2

ISBN–13 978-1-59811-855-1
ISBN–10 1-59811-855-2

MORMON PANTRY

Cooking with Food Storage

Made Easy

Debbie G. Harman

Hundreds of tasty, money-saving recipes
your family will love

Does the phrase "year's supply" or "food storage" frighten you? When I was young, my mind associated *food storage* with the end of the world, and I hoped that it would never really happen. Years later, as an adult with my own little family, those phrases continued to bring fear to my heart. But as my husband and I worked on obtaining our own food storage, I gained a whole new outlook.

We began by buying basic items for our storage. We had great ward leaders who helped us order and can food on a monthly basis. I learned how to grind wheat and make bread. In fact, I learned to make many things out of wheat. I found that I could save money by stocking up on sale items from the grocery stores. We started gardening and preserving foods from our harvest. Our family learned to become more self-sufficient. We gained a desire to live a more provident lifestyle, and I noticed that all this preparation gave me a feeling of peace. One day the thought came into my mind, "This counsel isn't to prepare us for the end of the world, it is to prepare us for *today.*"

There are many reasons to obtain a food supply. We never know what tomorrow will bring. But gathering food really is the easy part. We also need to know how to use it. Imagine having cars stored in your garage, but not knowing how to drive. When you know how to cook and use the basic storage foods, that is when you will feel prepared.

This book can help you learn how to cook and use basic storage foods. I hope you will gain confidence as you gather a year's supply of food and learn to use it. And I hope that through this experience your heart will be at peace when you hear the phrases "year's supply" and "food storage."

TABLE OF CONTENTS

I have often heard the phrase, "Store what you eat, and eat what you store." I must admit, whenever I hear that phrase I think of the story of Joseph, who was sold into Egypt by his brothers. The Lord helped Joseph prepare for a time when there would be a great famine in the land. Although we have seen "years of plenty" in our own lives, we have also seen times of crisis. We have witnessed many people throughout the world suffer because of natural disasters. Two years ago the price of wheat more than tripled because growers decided to produce corn instead of wheat, and today we are facing another economic crisis. We are always at risk, and it is only through our obedience to the Lord that we can have the promise that we will be protected.

You might not like wheat, rice, beans, and some of the other basic storage foods, so you may not feel the need to store them. Maybe you feel like you are wasting your money on foods you will never use. My advice would be to follow the simple guidelines the Church has given for these basic foods and to store them anyway. You and your family can learn to like wheat, rice, and beans if you need to, but if you don't have any of these stored it is almost certain that you *will* regret it. You can store some or all of the foods that you love, but make sure you have the basics in your storage as well!

Besides—after trying the recipes in this book, I am sure you will love the meals that you can make from these basic, easy-to-store foods!

STOCKING THE BASICS FOR FOOD STORAGE

Basic Storage Foods

Whole wheat	150 pounds per adult
Dry beans and legumes	60 pounds per adult
Rice	65 pounds per adult
Rolled oats	30 pounds per adult
Corn—dried, cornmeal,	30 pounds per adult
Pasta	10 pounds per adult
White flour	25 pounds per adult
Dry milk	24 pounds per adult
Sugar	40 pounds per adult
Honey	20 pounds per adult
Vegetable oil	10 quarts per adult
Salt	8 pounds per adult
Yeast	2 pounds per adult
Baking powder	1 pound per adult
Baking soda	1 pound per adult

These foods are considered the basic essentials and are the foods our leaders have counseled us to obtain. They are called *essential foods* because a person could survive on just these foods.

Other grains that you might want in your basic storage: Barley, farina, flaxseed, multiple grain mixtures, popcorn, and rye.

I also included pasta and white flour because they are often used in many recipes.

If you are just beginning your food storage program, I would suggest starting with one of each item, and then repeating the cycle. For example, the first thing you would get is one bag of wheat. Then the next week, buy a bag of beans. And the week after that, buy a bag of rice. Do this every week or month until you have one of everything on the list. You will soon find out how simple it is to follow this counsel, and it will bring peace and confidence into your heart to know you are prepared.

You will love the confidence you feel!

As soon as you begin stocking up on your storage, I would suggest that you begin using it. This is so important! This will help you get a better idea of how much your family uses. For example, we use a lot of wheat and cornmeal, but we use less oats and rice than are suggested.

We bought cans of the multigrain mixes when we first began, but I don't really use them. I have friends, however, that love them. Our family uses a lot of pinto and red beans, but not as many navy, northern, or lima beans.

Through using your storage foods, you will get a better feel for what you and your family will use.

This is not an excuse to say that you don't like any of these foods, so you are not going to store them.

There is a real purpose for us to store these foods, and you need to learn it!

STORAGE GUIDELINES

How to store food. If your storage foods are being used regularly, and are therefore being rotated, you shouldn't have any problems storing foods in the commercial packaging they come in. But problems can occur. Here are some solutions.

Weevils. Wheat, beans, sugar, honey, and dry milk should not have any problems. Rice, cornmeal, pasta, oats, and flour may have problems. If you are concerned, buy or seal foods in #10 cans at the dry-pack cannery. Contact your ward preparedness specialist for information. (If your foods do get weevils, you can still use them. But don't tell your kids!)

Flooding. Put bags inside buckets or store them on higher shelves. My suggested basic guidelines for all food storage items are:

Store in a cool and dry place.
Keep off the ground and away from any potential contamination.
Use foods daily to rotate them.

Iodized salt will keep weevils out of pasta. Place pasta in a container, and pour 1 C. salt over pasta. After you have used the pasta from the container, the salt may still be used.

Food Item	Shelf Life
Whole wheat	30 + years
Dry beans and legumes	30 + years
Rice	30 + years
Rolled oats	30 years
Corn—dried, cornmeal	30 years
Pasta (in the package)	12-18 months
White flour (in the bag)	12-18 months
Dry milk	10 + years
Sugar	Indefinite
Honey	Indefinite
Cooking oil	1 1/2-2 years
Salt	Indefinite
Yeast	1 year
Baking powder	Indefinite
Baking soda	Indefinite

"IN THE DAY OF PLENTY, PREPARE FOR THE DAY OF SCARCITY."

Message from the First Presidency, *Conference Report*, Apr. 1942

Other Basic Foods

After you have stored a supply of the essential basic foods, you may want to add other foods to your storage, such as:

Spices and condiments .... see Spice It Up section

Canned fruits and vegetables .... see Growing and Preserving for a Rainy Day section

Canned meats .... see Storing and Preserving Meats and Fish section

Dehydrated foods .... see Dehydrated Foods page

Seeds for gardening .... you will want to store both heirloom (will produce future seeds) and hybrid (won't produce future seeds)

You can also stock up on nonfood basics:
Pet foods, toothpaste, soap, lotion, shampoo, bathroom tissue, laundry and cleaning supplies, diapers, candles, fuel, first-aid supplies, medicines, sanitary supplies, etc.

Dehydrated Foods

Dehydrated foods have become increasingly popular in the food storage industry. There are so many foods to choose from, it would be impossible to give a list of suggested amounts. The following are the few that I feel would be most essential in a food storage program. Add to and adjust this list according to the specific tastes of your own family.

Food Item	Amount
Potatoes—sliced, diced, flakes	12-24 #10 cans
Onions—diced, minced	3-6 #10 cans
Vegetables	as per family needs
Dried whole eggs	6-12 #10 cans
Cheese powder	3-6 #10 cans
Sour cream powder	2-4 #10 cans
Buttermilk powder	1-2 #10 cans
Chicken gravy powder	2-4 #10 cans

And don't forget the water!

Plan for 7 gallons drinking water per person. Here are some tips:

    1. If buying water from stores, check the expiration dates, as the plastic does deteriorate. Look at the number inside the recycle triangle logo. The smaller the number, the stronger the plastic, and the longer it will last.

    2. To store tap water, use clean, heavy-duty plastic containers with tight-fitting lids. Store containers away from any fuels or chemicals.

The revelation to produce and store a food may be as essential to our temporal welfare today as boarding the ark was to the people in the days of Noah.

♥ Pres. Benson

Other Storage Items and Ideas

Other Storage Items and Ideas

_____

_____

_____

_____

_____

_____

_____

_____

_____

_____

_____

_____

_____

_____

_____

_____

The counsel to obtain and store an adequate supply of food has been given so that we may sustain life through any situation we may face. I believe it is extremely important to obey the counsel given to us. After all, the counsel has been given by prophets of God, and we know what can happen when their counsel is ignored. We cannot afford to ignore or alter this prophetic counsel.

After we obey and store that which has been asked of us, however, I believe it's up to us to use our own judgment as to how we use the food we store. This duty is ours, and the ability to make these foods taste good depends entirely on our own knowledge, experience, and skills. The way we prepare our storage foods will determine whether our family will like or dislike food storage.

The following pages list suggested condiments, seasonings, and spices that can be included in your storage. They are not required to sustain life; they are simply given as suggestions. Your list may be a little different according to your family's likes and dislikes. But I hope it will help you decide what you need to supplement your storage.

To me, these items are not the essentials, but they are the little extras that help us "spice it up!"

DON'T FORGET TO "SPICE IT UP"

Spice or Seasoning	Suggested Amount
Allspice	1-2 ounces
Basil	2-4 ounces
Bay leaves	2 ounces
Black pepper	4-6 ounces
Cayenne pepper	2 ounces
Celery seed	2-4 ounces
Chili powder	4-6 ounces
Chives	1-2 ounces
Cinnamon, ground	12-16 ounces
Cloves, ground	2-4 ounces
Cumin seed	2 ounces
Garlic, cloves, granulated, or powder	8-16 ounces
Ginger, ground	2-4 ounces
Italian seasoning	4-6 ounces
Lemon pepper	2 ounces
Mustard, dry	1 ounce
Nutmeg	2-4 ounces
Onions, minced or powder	12-16 ounces
Oregano	2-4 ounces
Parsley flakes	2-4 ounces
Paprika	2-3 ounces
Poppy seeds	6-8 ounces
Poultry seasoning	2 ounces
Seasoned salt	8-16 ounces
Sesame seeds	8-12 ounces

These amounts are suggested amounts for a family of six for one year. They are only approximate. Please adjust as you feel necessary.

Baking or Cooking Item	Suggested Amount
Canned milk	96-120 cans
Chocolate chips	4-10 pounds
Cornstarch	2-4 pounds
Corn syrup	2-4 quarts
Cocoa powder	2-4 pounds
Coconut, flaked	2-4 pounds
Cream of tartar	2 ounces
Extracts (almond, lemon, etc.)	4-8 ounces
Lemon juice	1-2 quarts
Malted milk powder	2-4 quarts
Maple flavoring (for syrup)	4-6 ounces
Molasses	1-4 quarts
Nuts (almonds, peanuts, pecans, walnuts, etc.)	12-20 pounds
Peanut butter	8-12 quarts
Shortening or lard	6-12 pounds
Sugar, brown	6-12 pounds
Sugar, powdered	6-12 pounds
Vanilla	1 quart

Baking items go on sale during the holiday season between October and December. It's a good time to stock up for the year. Flour, sugar, oil, nuts, raisins, chocolate chips, etc. are often as much as 1/3-1/2 off the regular prices. Be sure to check the expiration dates and only buy what you will use before foods expire.

15

Condiment or Flavoring	Suggested Amount
Apple cider vinegar	1 gallon
Barbecue, smoke, and other sauces	12-20 cups
Beef bouillon	16-24 ounces
Chicken bouillon	16-24 ounces
Cream soups	48-96 cans
Jell-O or other fruit gelatin mixes	12-24 packages
Ketchup	3-4 quarts
Mayonnaise or Miracle Whip	6-9 quarts
Mustard	1 pint
Olives, ripe	12-24 cans
Pickles and relish	4-8 pints
Punch powders for flavoring or drinks	12-48 packages
Popcorn	5-10 pounds
Powder mixes for gravies, soups, sauces, etc.	As needed
Salad dressings or dry mixes to make dressings	4-6 quarts
Soy sauce	1-3 quarts
Worcestershire sauce	1 pint

Other Storage Items

In addition to the basic foods for survival that we must have in our storage, it is wise to supplement that storage with fruits and vegetables.

Many prophets have counseled us that along with obtaining our one year's supply of basic survival foods, we should grow a garden and store the foods we grow. This section is about growing and preserving those foods.

The suggested amounts of preserved fruits and vegetables needed for one adult for a one-year supply are:

Citrus fruits and tomatoes (vitamin C)

1-cup serving per day ....65 quarts

Dark green and yellow vegetables (spinach, broccoli and other greens, carrots, yams, and yellow winter squash)

1/2-cup serving 4 times a week .... 20 quarts

Other fruits and vegetables (apples, apricots, cherries, peaches, pears, asparagus, corn, lima and green beans, peas, and summer squash)

1/2-cup serving 2 1/2 times per week .... 75 quarts

These amounts are from the USDA Daily Food Guide. I haven't included any amounts for jams, pickles, and relishes, so you will have to calculate those according to what your family uses.

You will want to use fresh produce in preparing meals whenever possible. The amounts listed above don't include the fresh produce your family will eat, but keep these amounts in mind as you are preserving foods for a rainy day.

GROWING AND PRESERVING FOR A RAINY DAY

Gardening

1. **Prepare your soil.** This begins in the Fall.

   Spread a 2-inch layer of broken-up leaves on your garden.

   Add nitrogen to leaves to help them decompose. Turn (plow) your soil.

   Add organic matter (manure) in the spring. Till the garden.

2. **Plan a watering system.** Plants depend on water.

3. **Plan your garden.** Map and record it so you can rotate plants each year. Keep a garden journal of failures and successes.

4. **Plant seeds inside** to have plants ready when ground is ready.

5. **Plant your garden.**

6. **Water and weed!**

PLANTING GUIDE

This guide is for the Wasatch Front; adjust it for your climate.

Vegetable	When to plant	Don't plant near these plants
Beans, pole - seed	May 5 - July 1	onion, beet, broccoli, cabbage, sunflower
Beets - seed	Mar 25 - July 15	pole bean
Broccoli - plant	Feb 15 - April 1	strawberry, pole bean, tomato
Cabbage - plant	Feb 15 - April 1	strawberry, pole bean, tomato
Carrot - seed	Mar 25 - June 15	
Cucumber - seed	May 5 - June 20	
Lettuce, leaf - seed	Mar 25 - May 15	
Onion - sets	Mar 15 - May 1	pole bean
Peas - seed	Mar 15 - May 1	onion, garlic, gladiolus, potato
Pepper - plant	May 20 - June 1	
Potato - piece	Mar 25 - May 15	pumpkin, tomato, cucumber, squash
Pumpkin - seed	May 1 - June 1	potato
Radish - seed	Mar 15 - Sept 1	
Spinach - seed	Mar 15 - May 1	
Squash, summer - seed	May 5 - July 1	potato
Squash, winter - seed	May 20 - June 1	
Corn, sweet - seed	May 5 - July 1	
Tomato - plant	May 1 - June 1	broccoli, cabbage, fennel, potato
Turnip - seed	Mar 15 - May 1	cabbage, fennel, potato

Canning Fruits

There is a time to plant and a time to harvest. Preserving foods is part of the "time to harvest." One of the ways we preserve fruits and vegetables is to bottle (can) them.

The following recipes are for altitudes between 3,000 and 6,000 feet.

1- Wash all jars, lids, and rings. (Only use jars that have been made for canning, and make sure they have no cracks or chips in the glass.)

2- Pack the fruit into the jars. There are basically two methods of packing: hot pack method (where fruit is cooked before packing) and raw pack method (where raw fruit is packed into jars). Make sure to leave space between the fruit and the top of the jar ("head space") when packing jars so the fruit doesn't bubble and spill over the top. Remove any air bubbles with a non-metal utensil (wooden spoon, rubber spatula, etc.).

3- Wipe the tops of jars and place lids on the jar mouths.

4- Screw the rings down firmly.

5- Place jars in the canner and process them according to the recipe.

6- Remove jars from the canner. When the jars are cool, make sure they are sealed by removing the ring and testing the lids. The lid should be firmly adhered to the jar and should have a slight concave in the center if sealed properly.

APPLESAUCE

1/2 bushel (24 lbs.) apples
3 C. granulated sugar

1/4 C. cinnamon (opt.)
7-9 quart jars and lids

Wash, drain, pare, quarter, and core apples. Place apples in large pot. Add 2 inches water and cover with lid. Simmer until apples are tender. Press apples through sieve or food processor. Return apples to pot. Add sugar and cinnamon (if desired). Bring apple mixture to a boil. Pour into hot jars. Leave 1/2-inch head space. Remove air bubbles, place lids and rings on jars, and tightly secure. Process 30 minutes in boiling water bath.

APPLE PIE FILLING

4 qts. water
6 C. granulated sugar
1/2 C. cinnamon (opt.)

3 Tbsp. ground nutmeg
1/2 bushel (24 lbs.) apples
8-10 quart jars and lids

Combine water and sugar in large pot and stir until sugar dissolves. Bring to a boil and boil 5 minutes. Add cinnamon and nutmeg. Wash, drain, pare, core, and slice (or chop) apples. Treat apples in Fruit Fresh or other solution to prevent darkening. Add apples to syrup and boil 5 minutes. Pour into hot jars. Leave 1/2-inch head space. Remove air bubbles, place lids and rings on jars, and tightly secure. Process 30 minutes in boiling water bath.

23

CHERRY PIE FILLING

4 qts. water
8 C. granulated sugar
1/4 C. cornstarch

1 C. water
6-8 qts. pie cherries, washed and pitted
8-10 quart jars and lids

Combine 4 qts. water and sugar in large pot and stir until sugar dissolves. Mix cornstarch with 1 C. water. Slowly stir cornstarch mixture into syrup. Cook over medium heat, stirring constantly, until mixture boils and thickens. Add cherries to syrup and boil 5 minutes. Pour into hot jars. Leave 1/2-inch head space. Remove air bubbles, place lids and rings on jars, and tightly secure. Process 30 minutes in boiling water bath.

BLACK CHERRIES

22 lbs. sweet cherries
4 C. sugar

5 qts. water
9-11 jars and lids

Wash, drain, and remove stems from cherries. Do not remove pits. Prick cherries with a sterilized needle so they won't burst. Combine water and sugar in large pot and stir until sugar dissolves. Bring to a boil and boil 5 minutes. Pour 1/2 C. syrup into hot jars. Fill jars with uncooked cherries. Jiggle jar to pack cherries well. Pour syrup over cherries. Leave 1/2-inch head space. Remove air bubbles, place lids and rings on jars, and tightly secure. Process 35 minutes in boiling water bath.

SLICED PEACHES

22 lbs. peaches
4 qts. water
4 C. sugar

5 qts. water
9-12 quart jars and lids

Wash and drain peaches. Heat about 4 qts. water in a large pot until boiling. Place 1/2 of the peaches in a wire basket or piece of cheesecloth and dip into boiling water for about 1 minute to loosen the skins. Dip peaches into cold water and drain. Repeat with remaining peaches. Cut peaches in half and remove skins and pits. Place peaches in Fruit Fresh or other solution to prevent darkening. Combine 5 qts. water and sugar in large pot and stir until sugar dissolves. Bring to a boil and boil 5 minutes. Pour 1/2 C. syrup into hot jars. Slice peaches and pack into jars. Pour hot syrup over peaches, leaving 1/2-inch head space. Remove air bubbles, place lids and rings on jars, and tightly secure. Process 40 minutes in boiling water bath.

PEAR HALVES

22 lbs. Bartlett pears
4 C. sugar

5 qts. water
9-12 quart jars and lids

Wash and cut pears in half; core and pare. Treat pears in Fruit Fresh or other solution to prevent darkening. Combine water and sugar in large pot and stir until sugar dissolves. Bring to a boil and boil 5 minutes. Cook pears in syrup 5 minutes. Pack hot pears into hot jars. Pour hot syrup over pears, leaving 1/2-inch head space. Remove air bubbles, place lids and rings on jars, and tightly secure. Process 35 minutes in boiling water bath.

WHOLE TOMATOES

21-24 lbs. tomatoes
4 qts. water
Lemon juice or citric acid

7 quart jars and lids
7 tsp. canning salt

Wash and drain tomatoes. In a large pot, bring 4 qts. water to a boil. Place tomatoes in a wire basket or piece of cheesecloth and dip into boiling water for about 30 seconds or until skins start to crack. Dip tomatoes into cold water and drain. Remove stems, skins, and any green or bad spots. Place whole tomatoes in a clean large pot. Cover with water and gently boil for 5 minutes. Remove prepared jars from hot water (one at a time so jars will stay hot) and drain. Place 2 Tbsp. lemon juice or 1/2 tsp. citric acid into jar. Pack hot tomatoes into hot jar, leaving 1/2-inch head space. Add 1 tsp. canning salt. Pour hot juice (from pot that tomatoes were cooked in) over tomatoes, leaving 1/2-inch head space. Remove air bubbles. Wipe jar top, place lid and ring on jar, and tightly secure. Place jar on rack in canner. Make sure canner is filled with hot, but not boiling, water. Repeat until all jars are filled with tomatoes. Make sure jars are covered with 2 inches of hot water. Cover canner with lid and bring water to a boil. Boil at a steady but gentle rate for 55 minutes. Remove jars from canner and place on cloth several inches apart where there won't be a draft. Cool for 12 hours. Remove bands and test seals. Store tomatoes in a cool, dark place.

WE WILL SEE THE DAY
WHEN WE WILL LIVE ON WHAT WE PRODUCE.
MARION G. ROMNEY

TOMATO SAUCE

45 lbs. tomatoes
7 tsp. salt

Lemon juice or citric acid
7 quart jars and lids

Wash and drain tomatoes. Remove stem and core. Cut into quarters. Simmer tomatoes, stirring occasionally, for 20 minutes. Press tomatoes through fine sieve or food mill. Cook and stir pulp over medium heat until thickened. Stir in salt. Place 2 Tbsp. lemon juice or 1/2 tsp. citric acid into each quart jar. Pour hot tomato sauce into hot jars, leaving 1/4-inch head space. Wipe jar top, place lid and ring on jar, and tightly secure. Place jar on rack in canner. Make sure canner is filled with hot, but not boiling, water. Repeat until all jars are filled with tomato sauce. Make sure jars are covered with 2 inches of hot water. Cover canner with lid and bring water to a boil. Process 50 minutes in boiling water bath.

TOMATO PASTE

Follow recipe and directions for tomato sauce, but continue cooking pulp until it thickens to a paste. Add only 1 Tbsp. salt. Use pint jars in place of quart jars. Place 1 Tbsp. lemon juice or 1/4 tsp. citric acid in each pint jar. Contiue as directed, but reduce processing time to 35 minutes.

APRICOT JAM

2 qts. crushed, peeled apricots
6 C. granulated sugar

1/4 C. lemon juice
5-6 pint jars and lids

Combine apricots, sugar, and lemon juice together in large saucepan. Bring mixture to a boil, stirring until sugar is dissolved. Cook over medium-high heat, stirring frequently, until mixture becomes thick (about 25 minutes). Pour hot jam into hot jars. Leave 1/4-inch head space. Remove air bubbles, place lids and rings on jars, and tightly secure. Process 25 minutes in boiling water bath.

PEACH JAM

2 qts. crushed, peeled peaches
1/2 C. water

6 C. granulated sugar
4-5 pint jars and lids

Combine peaches and water together in large saucepan and cook 10 minutes. Add sugar and bring mixture to a boil, stirring until sugar is dissolved. Cook over medium-high heat, stirring frequently, until mixture becomes thick (about 15 minutes). Pour hot jam into hot jars. Leave 1/4-inch head space. Remove air bubbles, place lids and rings on jars, and tightly secure. Process 25 minutes in boiling water bath.

STRAWBERRY JAM

2 qts. strawberries
2 tsp. grated lemon peel
1 tsp. lemon juice

1 pkg. powdered pectin
7 C. granulated sugar
4-5 pint jars and lids

Wash, drain, and hull strawberries. Crush enough strawberries to make 4 1/2 cups. Combine strawberries, lemon peel, lemon juice, and pectin together in a large saucepan. Bring to a rolling boil over high heat, stirring frequently. Add sugar and return to a full boil. Boil hard for 1 minute, stirring constantly. Pour hot jam into hot pint jars, leaving 1/4-inch head space. Remove air bubbles. Place lids and rings on jars and secure. Process 20 minutes in boiling water bath.

RASPBERRY JAM

2 qts. raspberries
1/3 C. water
2 tsp. grated lemon peel
1 Tbsp. lemon juice

1 pkg. powdered pectin
7 C. white sugar
4-5 pint jars and lids

Wash and drain raspberries. Follow rest of instructions as for straw-berry jam.

Vegetables

Vegetables are low-acid foods, so they must be canned in a pressure cooker. You will need a steam-pressure canner with either a dial gauge or a weighted gauge. All recipes in this section are based on an altitude between 4,000 and 6,000 feet. The pressure for a dial gauge is 13 psi, and a weighted gauge is 15 psi. Put 2-3 inches water in canner. Place jars in canner and put lid on canner and secure. Allow steam to escape through vent at a steady rate for 10 minutes before closing vent with gauge and begin timing.

COOKED CARROTS

20 lbs. carrots
Water

8-10 tsp. salt
8-10 quart jars and lids

Wash and peel carrots. Slice or dice carrots and place in large saucepan. Cover with water. Bring to a boil and simmer 5 minutes. Pack hot carrots into hot jars, leaving 1 inch of head space. Add 1 tsp. salt to each quart. Cover with boiling water, leaving 1-inch head space. Remove air bubbles, place lids and rings on jars, and tightly secure. Process 30 minutes in pressure canner.

WHOLE-KERNEL CORN

35 lbs. corn (in husks)
Water

7-10 tsp. salt
7-10 quart jars and lids

Husk corn cobs and remove silk. Wash corn and cut from cob. Pack corn loosely into hot jars, leaving 1 inch of head space. Add 1 tsp. salt per jar. Cover with boiling water, leaving 1-inch head space. Remove air bubbles, place lids and rings on jars, and tightly secure. Process 1 hour and 25 minutes in pressure canner.

CREAMED CORN

18 lbs. corn (in husks)
4-5 tsp. salt
Water

10-12 C. boiling water
8-10 pint jars and lids

Husk corn cobs and remove silk. Wash corn and cut the tips from the kernels. Scrape out pulp. Measure corn pulp as you put it into large saucepan. For each pint of corn pulp, stir in 1/2 tsp. salt and 1 1/4 C. water. Bring to a boil and boil 3 minutes. Pour hot mixture into hot jars, leaving 1 inch of head space. Remove air bubbles, place lids and rings on jars, and tightly secure. Process 1 hour and 25 minutes in pressure canner.

CUT GREEN BEANS

15 lbs. green beans
Water

3-4 tsp. salt
6-9 quart jars and lids

Wash and drain beans, removing any strings. Trim ends. Cut or break beans and place in large saucepan. Cover with water. Bring to a boil and boil 5 minutes. Pack hot beans into hot jars, leaving 1 inch of head space. Add 1/2 tsp. salt to each quart. Cover with boiling water, leaving 1-inch head space. Remove air bubbles, place lids and rings on jars, and tightly secure. Process 25 minutes in pressure canner.

"Grow vegetables and eat them from your own garden."

President Spencer W. Kimball

SUMMER SQUASH

25 lbs. summer squash
Water

3-4 tsp. salt
7-10 quart jars and lids

Wash but don't peel squash. Cut up squash and place in large saucepan. Cover with water. Bring to a boil and boil 2-3 minutes. Pack hot squash into hot jars, leaving 1 inch of head space. Add 1 tsp. salt to each quart. Cover with boiling water, leaving 1-inch head space. Remove air bubbles, place lids and rings on jars, and tightly secure. Process 40 minutes in pressure canner.

Frozen Foods

Another choice for preserving foods is freezing them. To freeze foods, you will need freezer bags or containers. Freezing foods is a good option, but storage space is limited and the storage life of the foods is not as long as that of canned foods. Also, with frozen foods, there is always the concern of the power going off. But even with all of these, there are some things that I like better frozen. Freezer jam and fresh fruits are among my favorites. I am not including any recipes for freezer jam, because they each call for powdered pectin and the recipes are included in the package of pectin. But I have included instructions for some of my other favorite frozen foods.

FROZEN APRICOTS

Wash and pit apricots. Place on cookie sheet or tray and place in freezer for 1 hour. Pack apricots into freezer bags, label, and return to freezer. When using apricots, remove only as many as you will use at that time.

These are perfect for making apricot smoothies.

FROZEN BERRIES

Wash, drain, and remove any stems from berries. Pat dry on paper towels. Place on cookie sheet or tray and freeze for 1 hour. Pack berries into freezer bags, label, and return to freezer. You can pack berries individually or combine different berries when packaging them.

We like strawberries packaged separately for strawberry smoothies, and we like a blend of berries as a fruit topping for yogurt.

FRUIT SMOOTHIES

1 C. milk   1 tsp. vanilla
1/4 C. sugar   Frozen fruit

Combine first three ingredients in a blender and add a few pieces of frozen fruit. Blend on high. Continue adding fruit and blending until desired thickness. Makes 2 servings.

FRUIT TOPPINGS

Place desired amount of frozen fruit in a glass bowl. Sprinkle 1/4 cup sugar for every cup of frozen fruit. Stir every couple of minutes until fruit starts to thaw. Sprinkle on yogurt, ice cream, or frosted cakes while partially frozen. This is also good for fruit pizza.

FROZEN PEACHES

Wash and drain peaches. Heat about 4 quarts water in a large pot until boiling. Place peaches in a wire basket or piece of cheesecloth and dip into boiling water for about 1 minute to loosen the skins. Dip peaches into cold water and drain. Cut peaches in half and remove skins and pits. Place peaches in Fruit Fresh or other solution to prevent darkening. Slice peaches and place in mixing bowl with measurements on the side. When you have nearly one quart, sprinkle 2/3 C. sugar over peaches and stir. Pack peaches into freezer bags, label, and freeze.

FROZEN PEAS

Shell and wash peas. Scald in hot water for 2 minutes. Cool and drain. Pack into 1-quart freezer bags, label, and freeze.

FROZEN CORN

Husk corn and remove silk. Wash and scald corn cobs 5-6 minutes. Cool, drain, and cut corn from the cob. Pack into freezer bags, label, and freeze.

Those families will be fortunate who, in the last days, have an adequate supply of food because of their foresight and ability to produce their own.

President Ezra Taft Benson

Dehydration

Dehydration (drying) is another way to preserve foods. Dried foods are easy to store and retain their flavor well. Foods can be sun-dried or air-dried in a warm room or dried in an oven, but a food dehydrator is the best and most economical way to dry foods. I have made fruit leather and sun-dried tomatoes in the oven, and it works, but it is costly to heat an oven. If you are going to be serious about drying foods, I would suggest getting a food dehydrator. They are available where small kitchen appliances are sold for about $40 to $60.

FRUIT LEATHER

2 C. applesauce   2 C. fresh fruit   1/4 C. sugar (opt.)

Wash, drain, and pit or seed fruit if needed. Place all ingredients together in a blender. Spread fruit sauce on drying trays. Dry 4-6 hours or until completely dried. Strawberries, plums, peaches, blueberries, raspberries, pears, and apricots work great for this recipe.

Cinnamon Apple: Use chopped apples for fruit, and add 1/2 tsp. cinnamon.

CHEWY STRAWBERRY FRUIT ROLLS

2 C. fresh strawberries
1/4 C. water

3 Tbsp. strawberry Jell-O powder
2 Tbsp. honey (opt.)

Wash and hull strawberries. Puree in blender, adding water if needed. Boil 1/4 C. water. Dissolve Jell-O powder and honey in water. Mix with strawberries. Spread on drying trays. Dry 4-5 hours until fully dried.

CHERRY FRUIT ROLLS

Follow above directions. Wash and pit cherries, measuring 2 C. cherries after they have been pitted. Use cherry-flavored Jell-O in place of the strawberry flavor. Dry as directed.

PLUM FRUIT ROLLS

4 C. plums, pitted
1/3 C. honey or corn syrup

1 Tbsp. lemon juice

Combine all ingredients in a blender and blend on high until thoroughly mixed. Spread fruit sauce on drying trays. Dry 4-6 hours or until completely dried.

DRIED FRUITS

Fruit	Preparation	Drying Time
Apples	Wash, core, and slice. Soak in pineapple or lemon juice for 1 hour.	6-12 hours
Apricots	Wash and pit; cut into quarters. Pre-treat as with apples.	12-16 hours
Bananas	Peel. Cut into 3/8-inch slices.	12-16 hours
Cherries	Wash. Remove stems and pits.	20-26 hours
Cranberries	Wash and remove stems. Blanch in boiling water until skins crack.	14-22 hours
Grapes	Wash and remove stems.	10-32 hours
Kiwi	Peel; cut into 3/8-inch slices.	13-16 hours
Mangos	Wash; remove pits and skins.	10-18 hours
Plums	Wash and pit plums.	12-20 hours
Strawberries	Cut in half or slice in 1/2-inch pieces.	10-14 hours

DRIED VEGETABLES

Vegetable	Preparation	Drying Time
Carrots	Wash, peel, and slice or grate.	8-12 hours
Celery	Wash and cut into 1/2-inch slices. Blanch in 1 C. water plus 1/2 tsp. soda.	6-10 hours
Corn	Husk corn and remove silk. Blanch and cut corn off cobs.	10-14 hours
Onions	Remove skins and cut into 3/8-inch slices.	9-13 hours
Peppers	Remove stems and seeds. Cut into 1/2-inch slices.	14-18 hours
Potatoes	Wash and cut into 3/8-inch slices.	6-10 hours

39

SUN-DRIED TOMATOES

2-3 lbs. tomatoes
1 C. olive oil
1 tsp. garlic powder

1/2 tsp. dried oregano
1/2 tsp. dried basil

Wash and remove stems from tomatoes. Slice tomatoes into eighths. Do not remove skins. Place tomatoes on drying trays. Dry 10-12 hours or until completely dried. Combine remainder of ingredients together in a quart jar. Pack dried tomatoes into jar. Refrigerate overnight before using. Store in refrigerator for up to 6 months.

FRENCH-FRIED ONIONS

4-5 large onions
1/4 C. vegetable oil

1/2-1 tsp. salt

Slice onions about 3/8-inch thick. Heat oil in large skillet. Saute onions until tender and transparent. Sprinkle with salt. Cool and place on drying trays. Dry 9-12 hours. Store in airtight container.

Use these for green bean casserole and other sauces and casseroles.

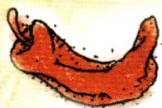

CHILI POWDER

4 oz. dried chilies
1 Tbsp. salt
2 tsp. garlic powder

1 tsp. onion powder
1 tsp ground oregano
1 tsp. ground cumin

Place dried chilies in a blender and blend until powdered. Add remaining ingredients and whirl just until blended. Store in plastic container.

This recipe can be used with any peppers, but remember that the hotter the pepper, the hotter the chili powder will be. Removing seeds from chilies before they are dried will decrease their hotness. You can add any seasonings you like to this recipe.

GROUND CORNMEAL

You can make your own cornmeal for cornbread, muffins, and other dishes from the corn you grow in your garden. Follow directions for drying corn in the dried vegetables guide. Grind dried corn in a wheat grinder. You can have course-ground or fine-ground flour. Home-ground cornmeal stays fresh only for about 3 days, so only grind the corn when you are going to use it right away.

Estimated savings of growing and preserving fruits and vegetables are between $100 and $200 per month, depending on the size and eating habits of your family.

Sprouting

You can have fresh greens in about 3 days by sprouting seeds in your own kitchen. Follow these simple directions.

1. Measure seeds and pick out any foreign objects.

2. Place seeds in a clean quart jar.

3. Fill jar half full with warm water. Remove seeds that float or sink.

4. Stretch gauze or nylon over top of jar and secure with rubber band.

5. Soak seeds for suggested time.

6. Drain seeds, leaving gauze on top of jar. Rinse in warm water. Drain again.

7. Follow step six 2-3 times a day so seeds won't sour.

8. When sprouts are ready, they can be eaten immediately.

9. Store sprouts in a tightly covered container and refrigerate.

SEED SPROUTING GUIDE

Seeds	Amount	Soak Time	Sprout Time	Length
Adzuki	1 C.	8-12 hours	4-5 days	1/2 - 1"
Alfalfa	3 Tbsp.	4-8 hours	3-5 days	1- 2"
Barley	2 C.	4-8 hours	3-4 days	1/4"
Pinto Bean	1 C.	8-12 hours	3-5 days	1"
Brown Rice	1 C.	8-12 hours	3-4 days	1/4"
Lettuce	3 Tbsp.	4-8 hours	3-5 days	1"
Mung Bean	1 C.	8-12 hours	3-5 days	1- 2"
Spinach	2 Tbsp.	6-8 hours	3-5 days	1/2-2"
Sunflower	1 C.	2-8 hours	1-2 days	1- 2"
Wheat	1 C.	8-12 hours	3-6 days	1/2"

Use sprouts in soups or salads. They can be used like lettuce on sandwiches or in tacos. Add them to bread, muffin, and bagel recipes. Bean sprouts are used in Chinese dishes like chow-mein and lo-mein. Sprouts can also be added to drinks or just eaten as a healthy snack.

Meats should be preserved and stored along with other basic storage items. There are basically three ways to store meats:

Freezing—This preserves the natural qualities of meat better than canning or drying. It's simple and easy to use when ready. The disadvantages of freezing meats are the risk of a power outage and the limitation on space.

Here are a few tips for freezing meat:

Packaging—Wrap meat tightly and remove all air pockets. If using zip-top bags, make sure air is pushed out of the bag before sealing.

Thawing—To thaw meat, place it in the refrigerator.
To thaw quickly, use the microwave defrost cycle, or try it mom's way—in a sink of cold water.

Refreezing—Refreeze meat only if part of the piece of meat is still frozen.

Drying—Check the recipes for jerky at the end of this section.

Canning—The recipes in this section are for canning meats. This may seem like a lot of work, but it will actually help you save time in the long run. If you take a few days a year to do the canning, you will have shelves filled with meats that have been cooked and are ready to be added to any casserole, soup, sauce, or sandwich.

PRESERVING AND STORING MEAT AND FISH

Poultry and Fish

The following recipes are for steam-pressure canners and altitudes between 4,000 and 6,000 feet. The pressure for these altitudes should be 15 psi. If your altitude is higher, the pressure should be higher, and lower altitudes should use lower pressure. Check the instruction guide that came with your canner. The temperature should be 240 degrees F.

BOTTLED CHICKEN

Chicken breast halves   Paprika
Chicken bouillon   Salt and pepper

Tightly pack raw chicken breast halves into jars, leaving at least 1-inch head space. Sprinkle 1 tsp. bouillon and a pinch of paprika, salt, and pepper over chicken. Wipe tops of jars, place lids and rings on jars, and tightly secure. Place jars in pressure canner with 2 inches water. Process 1 hour and 30 minutes at 15 psi.

Meat and poultry frequently go on sale. This is a good time to buy large quantities to can. You will save money and find it convenient to have cooked meats in your storage when making meals.

CHICKEN CHUNKS

7-8 lbs. chicken breast meat
5 C. water
5 tsp. chicken bouillon

Salt and pepper to taste
1 1/2 tsp. paprika

Cover chicken with water in a large pot. Sprinkle bouillon, salt, pepper, and paprika over chicken. Cover and cook on medium-low for 40-45 minutes or until chicken is tender. Remove chicken and cut into 1-inch chunks. Loosely pack chicken into jars, leaving 2-inch head space. Pour broth (from pot) over chicken, leaving 1-inch head space. If there isn't enough broth, fill with hot tap water, leaving 1-inch head space. Remove air bubbles. Wipe tops of jars, place lids and rings on jars, and tightly secure. Place jars in pressure canner with 2 inches water. Process 1 hour and 15 minutes at 15 psi.

CHICKEN SOUP

Follow the recipe for chicken chunks, but pack 2 chopped carrots, 2 chopped celery ribs, and 1/2 chopped onion in each jar with cooked chicken chunks. Sprinkle with 1 tsp. parsley flakes. Pour broth over chicken and vegetables, Leaving 1-inch head space. Continue as directed for canning.

Just heat up a quart or two, add noodles or rice, and you have quick homemade soup.

47

BOTTLED TURKEY

Turkey meat   Salt

Cut raw turkey meat into 1-inch chunks. Tightly pack turkey chunks into jars, leaving at least 1-inch head space. Tap bottle onto palm of your hand to help turkey meat settle. Pack in more meat if possible. Sprinkle 1 tsp. salt over turkey. Wipe tops of jars, place lids and rings on jars, and tightly secure. Place jars in pressure canner with 2-3 inches of water on bottom. Process 1 hour and 30 minutes at 15 psi.

Years ago I went to a camp meeting at the home of Annette Squire, who was the ward camp director. After the meeting, all of the girls and leaders gathered together for a nice lunch that she had prepared. The main dish of the meal was turkey salad sandwiches. They were delicious! About halfway through the meal, some girls showed up a little late, and all the sandwiches were gone. Annette wasn't stressed at all. She just brought out another bottle of turkey meat and made some more turkey salad. That really strengthened my belief in food storage. I could see how Annette's efforts to have an adequate food storage had brought simplicity into her everyday life.

You can make turkey salad by mixing Miracle Whip with the drained bottled turkey chunks. If desired, add a little relish. It's wonderful!

BOTTLED FISH

Prepare fish as you would for cooking. Fish should be soaked in salt water before canning. Only use pint jars to can your fish, because it is very low in acidity and heat may not be able to penetrate all of the meat to destroy the bacterial spores when packed into larger jars. Remove the backbone from large fish, but leave it in small fish. Process pints in a pressure canner 1 hour and 40 minutes at 15 pounds psi.

Beef and Pork

BEEF CHUNKS

Cut raw beef into 1-inch chunks. Tightly pack beef chunks into jars, leaving at least 1-inch head space. Tap bottle onto palm of your hand to help meat settle. Pack in more meat if possible. Sprinkle 1 tsp. salt over beef chunks. Wipe tops of jars, place lids and rings on jars, and tightly secure. Place jars in pressure canner with 2-3 inches of water on bottom. Process 1 hour and 30 minutes at 15 psi.

Pork Chunks: Follow directions for beef chunks, using a raw pork roast.

HEARTY BEEF STEW

1 C. all-purpose flour
10-12 lbs. beef stew meat
1/3 C. vegetable oil
18 carrots, peeled and sliced
18 potatoes, peeled and cubed

4 onions, chopped
12 celery ribs, sliced
1 Tbsp. garlic powder
1/3 C. beef bouillon
10 C. water

Put flour in large bag. Cut stew meat into 1-inch cubes. Shake a few pieces of meat to coat. Heat 2 Tbsp. oil in large pot. Brown meat. Continue coating meat with flour and browning meat until all pieces have been browned. Place meat and remaining ingredients in pot. Bring to a boil. Reduce heat, cover and simmer 30 minutes. Follow processing directions for beef chunks.

You can also follow these recipes for pork, chicken, or turkey.

SHREDDED BEEF

Rub beef bouillon or kitchen bouquet on roast. Place roast in Crock-Pot. Cover and cook on high for 3-4 hours or until beef falls apart. Shred beef using two forks and pulling beef apart. Pack beef into jars leaving 2-inches head space. Pour broth from pot over beef, leaving 1-inch head space. If there isn't enough broth, fill with hot tap water, leaving 1-inch head space. Process following directions for beef chunks.

BOTTLED HAM

Cut ham into 1/2-inch chunks. Tightly pack ham into jars, leaving at least 1-inch head space. Tap bottle onto palm of your hand to help ham settle. Pack in more meat if possible. Cover ham with water, leaving 1-inch head space. Wipe tops of jars, place lids and rings on jars, and tightly secure. Place jars in pressure canner. Process 1 hour and 30 minutes at 15 psi.

This ham is perfect for soups, casseroles, and Chinese dishes. It's also great for salads and sandwiches.

Meat Sauces

SLOPPY JOE SAUCE

10 lbs. hamburger
Salt and pepper to taste
3 envelopes Sloppy Joe seasoning mix
2 carrots, peeled and grated
4 stalks celery, finely diced

3 onions, finely chopped
2 C. ketchup
3/4 C. sugar
3 qts. tomato sauce

Brown meat with salt and pepper. Drain fat. Stir in remaining ingredients and simmer 30 minutes. Pour hot sauce into hot jars, leaving 1-inch head space. Wipe jars and place lids and rings on and tightly secure. Place jars in pressure canner. Process 1 hour and 30 minutes at 15 psi.

SPAGHETTI SAUCE

3 lbs. sweet Italian sausage
7 lbs. ground beef
Salt and pepper to taste
6 garlic cloves, minced
1/2 C. sugar

1/4 C. Italian seasoning
4 16-oz. cans tomato sauce
2 qts. crushed tomatoes
3 4-oz. cans mushrooms (opt.)

Brown meats together in a large soup pot, seasoning with salt, pepper, and garlic. Drain fat. Add remaining ingredients. Simmer uncovered for 30 minutes, stirring occasionally and skimming off fat as it surfaces. Pour hot spaghetti sauce into hot quart jars, leaving 1-inch head space. Wipe tops of jars, place lids and rings on jars, and tightly secure. Place jars in pressure canner. Process 1 hour and 30 minutes at 15 psi.

If desired, you can replace the sausage with hamburger. You can also substitute 2 Tbsp. garlic powder for the garlic cloves.

MEXICAN CHILI

7 lbs. lean ground beef
Salt and pepper to taste
2 garlic cloves, minced
3 medium onions, chopped
1 hot red pepper, finely chopped

1/2 C. chili powder
1 Tbsp. salt
1 1/2 tsp. cumin seed
2 qts. tomatoes

Brown meat with salt, pepper, and garlic. Drain fat. Add remaining ingredients. Simmer for 20 minutes. Skim off fat as it surfaces. Pour hot chili into hot quart jars, leaving 1-inch head space. Remove air bubbles. Wipe tops of jars, place lids and rings on jars, and tightly secure. Place jars in pressure canner. Process 1 hour and 30 minutes at 15 psi.

Dried Jerky

BARBECUED BEEF JERKY

3 lbs. lean beef
1/4 C. brown sugar
2 tsp. dry mustard
1 tsp. onion powder
2 Tbsp. Worcestershire sauce

1 C. ketchup
1/4 C. vinegar
1 tsp. salt
1/4 tsp. cracked pepper
1 tsp. hot pepper sauce

Cut beef into strips 1/2-inch thick. Combine remaining ingredients in large dish. Add beef strips. Cover and refrigerate overnight. Drain slices and dry in food dehydrator at 145 degrees until pliable. Store in jars or storage bags.

SOY BEEF JERKY

3 lbs. lean beef
1/4 C. brown sugar
3/4 C. soy sauce
1/4 C. Worcestershire sauce

1 tsp. garlic powder
1 tsp. onion powder
1/4 tsp. cracked pepper
1/4 tsp. liquid smoke

Follow the preparation and drying directions in Barbecued Beef Jerky.

Last summer we took the youth of our stake on the Martin-Willey hand-cart trek. We had to decide if we would let them experience the real hardships these pioneers faced (feed them flour cakes and let them go hungry). We decided they would be happier if we fed them good meals, so we found the best cooks in Manti to feed our youth while they were trekking, and they ate well! Even though the trek was extremely difficult and they faced many other challenges, they were so positive and happy. Our trek was a huge success! I know the delicious and nutritious food was the key to our youth and leaders being so happy. This taught me an amazing lesson . . .

You can handle almost anything if you are "well fed."

 We should remember this same principle as we plan and use our food storage. If you have an adequate food storage *and* you can prepare delicious meals, your family will be more likely to survive anything.

We must realize, however, that if we are faced with challenging times as the handcart companies were, we will have to survive on only the foods we have with us. We may not be able to run to the store for a gallon of milk and a dozen eggs. It is with these times in mind that I have written this section. It isn't easy to make meals with dehydrated cheese and sour cream when you are used to using fresh dairy products, but I think it is wise to practice making foods that will sustain us and taste good to us should we be faced with this situation in our lives.

I hope you can find some recipes in this section that your family will enjoy. I hope you will never be forced to live on your storage alone, but should it happen, being prepared will keep you and your family happy through the challenges because you will be "well fed."

MAIN AND SIDE DISHES

Meat-n-Potatoes

HAM-N-CHEESE POTATOES

3 C. dried potato slices
1 qt. water
Salt and pepper to taste
1/2 C. cheese powder

1 C. water
1/2 qt. bottled ham
1 can evaporated milk
2 Tbsp. chives

Spread potato slices in a greased casserole dish. Boil water and pour over potatoes. Sprinkle with salt and pepper. Bake at 350 for 30-40 minutes or until potatoes are tender. Stir cheese powder into 1 C. water until smooth. Pour over potatoes. Stir in ham and canned milk. Sprinkle with chives. Bake an additional 20 minutes to heat through.

HAM-BROCCOLI POTATOES

Follow directions for Ham-N-Cheese Potatoes, but add 1-2 C. chopped broccoli when you add the ham. Continue as directed.

SCALLOPED POTATOES

3 C. dried potato slices
Water
1- 2 C. dried onions

Salt and pepper to taste
Unbleached white flour
2 cans evaporated milk

Boil potatoes in water to cover until tender. Drain. Spread a thin layer of potatoes in a greased 9 x 13 casserole dish. Sprinkle with dried onions, salt, pepper, and flour. Repeat layers until all potatoes have been used. Pour canned milk over potatoes. Bake at 350 for 30-40 minutes.

CHICKEN AND POTATOES

1 qt. chicken chunks
3 C. dried potato slices
1 qt. green beans

1/2 C. sour cream powder
3 C. water
Salt and pepper to taste

Combine chicken, potatoes, and green beans in Crock-Pot. Add 2 C. water. Mix sour cream powder with remaining water until smooth. Pour over chicken and potatoes. Sprinkle with salt and pepper. Cook on high 1-2 hours or until potatoes are tender.

For variety, substitute carrots for the green beans.

This recipe can also be cooked in the oven. Combine all ingredients in a casserole dish. Bake at 350 for 1 hour or until potatoes are tender.

YUMMY POTATOES

3 C. dried potato slices
1/4 C. minced onions
1 can evaporated milk
1/2 C. sour cream powder

1/4 C. cheese powder
1 can cream of chicken soup
1 C. water
1 C. crushed corn flakes

Boil potatoes and onions until tender. Drain. In a 9 x 13 baking dish, combine evaporated milk, sour cream and cheese powders, chicken soup, and water. Stir in potatoes and onions. Sprinkle corn flakes over top. Bake at 350 for 30-40 minutes.

You can make your own corn flakes from the recipe in the Cooking with Wheat and Grains section.

"Begin in a small way . . .
and gradually build toward a reasonable objective."

President Gordon B. Hinckley

OVEN-FRIED POTATOES

2 C. dried potato slices
1/2 tsp. salt
1/4 C. cooking oil

1/4 tsp. garlic powder
1/4 tsp. paprika
Salt and pepper to taste

Boil potatoes and 1/2 tsp. salt until tender. Drain. Thinly spread potatoes on sheet-cake pan. Mix remaining ingredients, and brush mix on potatoes. Bake at 425 for 15-20 minutes or until golden brown.

CHEESY BARBECUE-FRIED POTATOES

Follow directions for Oven-Fried Potatoes. After potatoes are golden brown, remove potatoes from oven. Spread your favorite barbecue sauce over potatoes. Sprinkle with shredded cheddar cheese or prepared cheese sauce. Return to oven. Bake for 5-10 minutes or until cheese is melted.

BACON-N-ONION-FRIED POTATOES

Follow recipe for Oven-Fried Potatoes, but sprinkle minced onions and bacon bits over potatoes before baking. Continue as directed.

GARLIC MASHED POTATOES

4 C. potato flakes
1/4 C. vegetable oil
1 tsp. salt

1/4 C. sour cream powder
1 can evaporated milk
1/2 tsp. garlic powder

Make mashed potatoes according to package directions. Combine remaining ingredients. Stir into potatoes until well blended.

BACON-MASHED POTATOES

Follow directions for Garlic Mashed Potatoes, but replace garlic powder with 1/2 C. bacon bits.

MASHED POTATOES AND CHICKEN GRAVY

4-6 C. mashed potatoes
1 qt. chicken chunks
1/4 C. flour

1 can evaporated milk
Salt and pepper to taste

Cook potatoes according to package directions. For gravy, combine remaining ingredients in a large saucepan. Cook and stir over medium-high heat until thickened and bubbly. Season with salt and pepper.

60

POWDERED MILK GRAVY

1 C. powdered milk
1/4 C. flour
3 C. water

1 tsp. salt
2 Tbsp. vegetable oil

Combine powdered milk and flour in a medium saucepan. Slowly stir in 3 C. water. Add salt and vegetable oil. Cook and stir over medium heat until gravy thickens. If desired, stir in 1/4 tsp. black pepper. Serve over steamed green peas, mashed potatoes, toast, or biscuits.

You can also make this gravy using any meat drippings. Substitute drippings for the vegetable oil.

Dehydrated potatoes have a shelf life of 30 or more years, making them a good item for your food storage.

CORNED BEEF HASH

2 C. dried diced potatoes
1 C. dried diced onions
1/4 C. powdered milk
1 1/2 tsp. salt

1/4 tsp. pepper
5 C. water
3 Tbsp. vegetable oil
2 cans corned beef

Combine first 6 ingredients in a large pot. Boil for 10-15 minutes or until water is mostly absorbed. Heat oil in skillet. Add potatoes and begin cooking. Stir in corned beef. Cook, turning frequently, 20 minutes or until potatoes are browned.

SLOPPY-BEAN JOES

1 qt. Sloppy Joe sauce
2 C. cooked red beans
12-16 rolls or buns

Combine Sloppy Joe sauce and beans in a medium saucepan. Simmer 10-15 minutes. Slice rolls or buns and fill with sauce. (Heavenly Surprise Dinner Rolls from the Cooking with Wheat section are great for Sloppy Joes.)

You can also use rice as an extender for Sloppy Joes. Mix in 1 C. cooked rice for every qt. sauce.

SHEPHERD'S PIE

3 C. dried potato slices   Salt and pepper
1 qt. mixed vegetables   Paprika

Boil potatoes until tender. Drain. Drain vegetables and pour into a greased 9 x 13 casserole dish. Spread potatoes over vegetables. Sprinkle with salt, pepper, and paprika. Bake at 350 for 30-40 minutes.

Green Shepherd's Pie: Spread 1 16-oz. bag frozen peas in a greased 9 x13 casserole dish. Top with potato slices or mashed potatoes. Sprinkle with salt, pepper, and paprika. Bake at 350 for 30 minutes.

BEEF POT PIES

1 qt. beef chunks	1 C. frozen peas and carrots
1/4 C. diced dried onions	1/4 C. flour
1 C. diced dried potatoes	Pie crust dough for 2 pies

Combine first four ingredients with 2 C. water in a large saucepan. Simmer, uncovered, until potatoes are tender. Meanwhile, make pie crust according to directions. (See pie crust recipe in Snacks and Treats section.) Roll out dough and cut into 6-inch squares. Using a slotted spoon, place about 1/3 C. beef filling in center of each square. Fold one corner across to opposite corner to make a triangle. Pinch edges to seal. Carefully place pot pies on greased baking sheet. Bake at 375 for 25-30 minutes or until crust is golden brown.

CHICKEN POT PIES

Follow recipe for Beef Pot Pies, replace the beef chunks with 1 qt. chicken chunks. Continue as directed.

TURKEY POT PIES

Follow recipe for Beef Pot Pies, but replace beef chunks with 1 qt. turkey chunks. Continue as directed.

Pasta Dishes

MACARONI AND CHEESE

2 C. dry macaroni noodles
1/2 C. cheese sauce powder

1 can evaporated milk
1 C. water

Cook macaroni according to package directions. Drain. Return to pan. Add remaining ingredients and stir until well blended.

HAM-N-CHEESE MACARONI

Follow recipe for Macaroni and Cheese. Cut 1 lb. ham into 1/2-inch cubes. Fry ham cubes in a skillet until browned on all sides. Mix with macaroni and cheese.

Research shows that these common longer-term food storage items, such as macaroni, remain nutritious and edible much longer than previously thought if they are properly stored at or below room temperature (75 degrees F; 24 degrees C). Macaroni, along with many other basic storage items, is estimated to have a shelf-life of 30 years. *Ensign,* March 2009

TOMATO MACARONI BAKE

3 C. dry macaroni noodles
1/2 C. cheese sauce powder
1 qt. stewed tomatoes

1 can evaporated milk
2 Tbsp. vegetable oil
2 C. whole-kernel corn

Cook macaroni according to package directions. Drain. Turn into a 9 x 13 baking pan. Add remaining ingredients and stir until well blended. Sprinkle with salt and pepper. Bake at 425 for 25 minutes.

BEEF STROGANOFF

2 lbs. ground beef
Salt, pepper, and garlic powder to taste
1 can cream of mushroom soup
2 Tbsp. Worcestershire sauce

1 can evaporated milk
3 Tbsp. sour cream powder
1/4 C. water

Brown ground beef with salt, pepper, and garlic powder. Drain fat. Stir remaining ingredients into browned meat. Simmer until heated through. Serve over hot cooked egg noodles.

WHEAT STROGANOFF

Boil 1 C. wheat with 1 tsp. beef bouillon and 1/2 tsp. salt in 3 C. water until softened (about 1 hour). Drain wheat. Add to Beef Stroganoff recipe to extend meat, or replace ground beef with cooked wheat.

EASY SPAGHETTI

Spaghetti noodles
1/2 tsp. oregano

1 qt. spaghetti sauce
Parmesan cheese (opt.)

Cook spaghetti according to package directions. Drain. Combine oregano with bottled spaghetti sauce. Warm through. Serve over cooked noodles. If desired, sprinkle with Parmesan cheese.

Serve with soft whole-wheat breadsticks from Cooking with Whole and Other Grains section.

CHICKEN SPAGHETTI

Place cooked spaghetti noodles in a 9 x 13 casserole dish. Spread 1 qt. chicken chunks over noodles. Spread meatless sauce over chicken and noodles. If desired, sprinkle with Parmesan cheese. Bake at 350 for 20-30 minutes or until cheese is golden.

Baked Spaghetti

Put cooked noodles and sauce in a 9 x 13 baking pan. Sprinkle with Parmesan cheese. Bake at 425 for 25 minutes.

WHEAT SPAGHETTI SAUCE

1 C. whole wheat
1/2 tsp. salt
3 C. water
2 lbs. ground beef
Salt, pepper, and garlic powder to taste
1 Tbsp. garlic powder

2 Tbsp. sugar
1 Tbsp. Italian seasoning
2 8-oz. cans tomato sauce
1 qt. crushed tomatoes
1 4-oz. can mushrooms (opt.)

Boil wheat and 1/2 tsp. salt in 3 C. water until softened (about 1 hour). Drain. Brown meat with salt, pepper, and garlic powder. Drain fat. Add the wheat and remaining ingredients. Simmer 30-40 minutes.

Boiled wheat can be used to extend or replace meat. Just follow above recipe, but substitute meat with one additional can mushrooms.

BAKED LASAGNA

12 lasagna noodles
1 1/2 C. spinach flakes (opt.)
1/3 C. sour cream powder
1/4 C. cheese powder

1 can evaporated milk
1/2 C. Parmesan cheese
1 Tbsp. parsley flakes
1 qt. spaghetti sauce

Cook lasagna noodles and drain. Combine next 6 ingredients to make cheese filling. Place a layer of 3 noodles in a greased 9x13 baking dish. Spread 1/3 cheese mixture on noodles. Spread 1 C. sauce over cheese. Repeat layers. Top with remaining noodles, sauce, and sprinkle with Parmesan cheese. Bake at 350 for 30 minutes.

GOULASH

3 C. macaroni, cooked
1 qt. tomatoes
2 C. green beans
2 C. corn

1 16-oz. can kidney beans
2 C. grated cheese
Salt and pepper to taste

Combine noodles, vegetables, and beans in a 9 x 13 casserole dish. Sprinkle with grated cheese, salt, and pepper. Bake at 350 for 30 minutes.

. . . there arose a mighty famine in the land; and he began to want.

Luke 15:14

TUNA-MAC CASSEROLE

1 C. dried potato slices
2 Tbsp. vegetable oil
Salt to taste
4 C. macaroni, cooked

2 small cans tuna
1 can cream of mushroom soup
1 can evaporated milk
2 C. peas, frozen or canned

Cook potatoes in boiling water until just tender. Drain well. Heat oil in large skillet. Cook potatoes in hot oil until crispy and golden brown. Sprinkle salt over fried potatoes. Mix remaining ingredients in a 9 x 13 casserole dish. Sprinkle fried potatoes on top. Bake at 350 for 30 minutes.

Rice and Corn

BEEF AND RICE

2 C. brown or white rice
1 qt. beef chunks
1 qt. green beans, drained

1 can cream of mushroom soup
1/4 C. minced onions
Salt and pepper

Cook rice according to package directions (or use the Basic Cooked Rice recipe in the Cooking with Whole Wheat and Other Grains section). Add remaining ingredients and heat through. Season with salt and pepper.

TURKEY AND RICE

Follow directions for the Beef and Rice recipe, but replace beef with 1 qt. turkey chunks, and replace the cream of mushroom soup with cream of chicken soup. Continue as directed.

If you do not have bottled meat, you can use 2 C. cooked and drained beans in these recipes.

VEGETABLE RICE PILAF

1/4 C. oil or butter
2 C. brown or white rice
3/4 C. green onion, chopped
3/4 C. celery, diced

3/4 C. carrots, diced
4 tsp. chicken bouillon
4 C. water
1/2 C. bacon bits (opt.)

Heat oil in large saucepan. Add rice and saute until browned. Combine remaining ingredients except bacon bits with rice. Sprinkle with salt and pepper. Cover and reduce heat. Simmer 20-30 minutes or until rice and vegetables are tender. Stir in bacon bits if desired. Bake at 350 for 30 minutes.

BROWN AND WILD RICE PILAF

1 4-oz. can mushrooms, drained
1/2 C. green onions, chopped
1 Tbsp. vegetable oil
3 1/2 C. water
3 tsp. chicken bouillon
1 C. brown rice

1/2 C. wild rice
1/2 tsp. dried basil
1/8 tsp. black pepper
1/2 C. frozen peas
1 carrot, shredded

In a large saucepan, saute mushrooms and green onions in hot oil until tender. Add water and bouillon and bring to a boil. Add brown and wild rice, basil, and pepper. Cover and reduce heat. Simmer 40 minutes or until rice is tender and most of the broth is absorbed. Stir in peas and carrots and simmer 5 minutes or until heated through.

TUNA-RICE CASSEROLE

2 C. rice, cooked
2 cans tuna

1 can cream of mushroom soup
2 C. green beans, drained

Cook rice according to package directions (or follow directions from Basic Rice recipe in the Cooking with Whole Wheat and Other Grains section). Add remaining ingredients and heat through. Season with salt and pepper.

HERB-SEASONED RICE

2 Tbsp. butter or oil
1/4 C. onion, finely diced
1 clove garlic, minced
2 green onions, chopped
1 C. long-grain rice

2 C. water
2 tsp. chicken bouillon
1 tsp. Italian seasoning
2 Tbsp. parsley flakes
1 bay leaf

Melt butter in medium saucepan. Saute onion, garlic, and green onion until garlic is golden. Add rice and stir until coated with butter. Add water, bouillon, and herbs. Bring to a boil. Cover with tight-fitting lid. Reduce heat to low and simmer 20 minutes. Remove bay leaf.

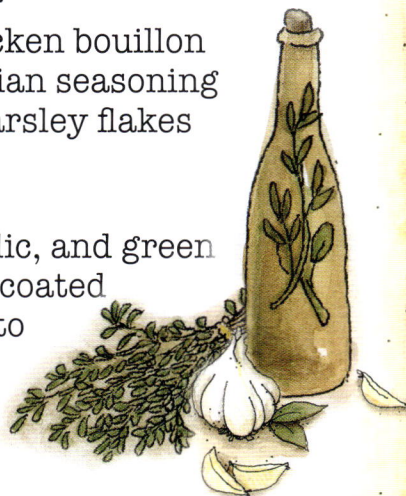

Rice is great as a side dish or as an ingredient in main dishes. With a cost of less than 10 cents a serving and having a very long shelf life, rice is a great item for your food storage.

HAM-FRIED RICE

2 Tbsp. vegetable oil
3 Tbsp. reconstituted eggs
1/2 C. ham, diced
2 C. day-old cooked rice

2 green onions, chopped
1/2 C. peas and carrots
1/2 tsp. chicken bouillon
2 tsp. soy sauce

Heat 1 Tbsp. oil in a large skillet. Scramble eggs. Remove eggs from skillet and heat remaining oil. Stir-fry ham and rice (day-old rice works best because it is drier than fresh-cooked rice) until ham starts to brown. Add green onions, peas, and carrots, and stir-fry until vegetables are cooked through. Sprinkle with bouillon and soy sauce. Return scrambled eggs to skillet and mix well.

SPANISH RICE

3 C. cooked rice
1/4 C. minced onions
1/2 C. bacon bits
1 tsp. chili powder

1 qt. diced tomatoes
1 4-oz. can diced green chilies
1 16-oz. can corn, drained
1 C. mild cheese, grated (opt.)

Mix all ingredients except cheese in a 9 x 13 baking dish. Sprinkle cheese over top. Bake at 350 for 30 minutes or until cheese is melted and bubbly.

MEXICAN CORNBREAD

2 C. all-purpose flour
1 C. cornmeal
2 Tbsp. baking powder
1 tsp. salt
2 Tbsp. dried egg powder

1/4 C. powdered milk
1/2 C. vegetable oil
2/3 C. water
1 4-oz. can diced green chilies
1/2 C. whole-kernel corn

Grease a 9 x 13 baking pan and line the bottom with waxed paper. In a large bowl, sift dry ingredients together, including egg powder and powdered milk. Whisk oil and water together. Pour into dry ingredients. Add the green chilies and corn and mix well. Pour into prepared pan. Bake at 400 for 20-25 minutes, or until lightly browned.

CHILI CORNBREAD CASSEROLE

1 qt. Mexican Chili (see recipe in
    Preserving Meats section)

2 C. red beans, cooked (opt.)
1 recipe Mexican Cornbread

Spread Mexican chili and, if desired, red beans in a 9 x 13 baking dish. Prepare Mexican Cornbread as directed in recipe. Spread over chili. Bake at 400 for 30-35 minutes or until cornbread is cooked at the center.

Any chili or chili beans may be used in this recipe.

COWBOY CORNBREAD

1 recipe cornbread   1 qt. beef stew

Follow recipe for cornbread from the Cooking with Whole Wheat and Other Whole Grains section. Spread beef stew (with juice) in a 9 x 13 baking dish. Top with cornbread batter. Bake at 350 for 25-30 minutes or until cornbread is thoroughly cooked at the center.

TAMALE PIE

2 C. corn masa (corn flour)   1-1 1/4 cups water
1/4 C. shortening   1 qt. shredded beef (or
1/2 tsp. salt   3 C. refried beans)
2 Tbsp. hot sauce   1 C. sliced ripe olives (opt.)

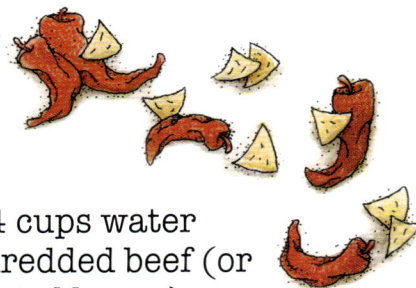

Combine corn masa, shortening, and salt together. Stir in hot sauce and water until a thick paste forms. Spread 1/2 of the masa paste in a greased 9 x13 baking dish. Spread shredded beef, beans, or a mixture of both over the masa. If desired, sprinkle with sliced olives. Top with remaining masa paste. Cover with foil or lid. Bake at 350 for 35-45 minutes or until masa is firm and cooked through.

The average shopper spends at least $10 on splurge and impulse items (foods and treats that aren't necessities) every shopping trip. Using food storage prevents many of those shopping trips, which can equal a savings of $40 or more per month.

ENCHILADAS

2 C. cooked rice
3 C. pinto or black beans
12 corn tortillas
1 tsp. chili powder
1 Tbsp. onion powder

2 tsp. garlic powder
1 4-oz. can diced green chilies
1 qt. tomatoes or sauce
1 C. grated cheese or 1/4 C.
cheese sauce powder

Combine rice and beans. Place 1/3 C. bean mixture in each corn tortilla and roll up. Place filled tortillas in a 9 x 13 baking dish. In a blender, combine the spices, green chilies, and tomatoes until pureed. Pour sauce over tortillas. Bake at 350 for 30 minutes. Sprinkle grated cheese or prepared cheese sauce (follow package directions) over top and return to oven until cheese is melted and bubbly.

SMOTHERED BURRITOS

2 Tbsp. vegetable oil
3 Tbsp. flour
2 4-oz. cans diced green chilies
1 qt. pork chunks

1 tsp. chili powder
1/2 tsp. chicken bouillon
12 corn or flour tortillas
3 C. refried beans

Heat 2 Tbsp. oil in a large skillet. Stir in flour to make a thick paste. Add pork chunks (juice included), green chilies, chili powder, and chicken bouillon. Cook and stir over medium heat until thickened and bubbly. Spread 1/2 cup refried beans in each tortilla. Fold up burrito style. Place burritos in greased 9 x 13 baking dish. Cover with sauce. Bake at 350 for 30-40 minutes or until sauce is bubbly.

Beans and legumes, along with grains, have an important role in a complete food storage program.

Animal proteins (including meat and dairy) are complete proteins, but two vegetable proteins combined will also make a complete protein. Beans combined with another vegetable protein—such as wheat, barley, or rice—make a complete protein and can substitute for meat. Although meat is a very important substance in our diet during times of famine, it is sometimes not available. If you have little meat in your storage, you can make sure your family is getting enough protein if you are serving beans and legumes with your grains.

Many of the recipes in this section are slow-cooked in a Crock-Pot, but all of them can be cooked in a stock or soup pot on the stove. Also, if you're in a hurry, there are quick ways to cook beans. These methods will be discussed in this section.

Some of the recipes in this section call for dried foods, while others call for fresh meats, produce, and dairy products. In reality, sometimes we have fresh foods and other times we don't. It's always best to use fresh foods, but it is also important to know how to use preserved foods so we will be prepared when fresh foods aren't available. I would suggest using variety. If you make a meal with dried foods one night, use fresh the next night. All of these recipes can be made with fresh or dried foods, so feel free to make substitutions wherever needed.

I hope you will enjoy making beans, soups, and stews part of your food storage experience.

BEANS, SOUPS, AND STEWS

Dry Beans
and Lentils

Beans are nutritionally very important in the diet and are very high in protein, carbohydrates, iron, and B vitamins. Beans are one of the richest sources of fiber. They are low in fat (only 2-3 percent) and have no cholesterol. They are inexpensive, easy to store, and have a very long shelf life. Beans are definitely a must in a good food storage program.

Here are a few ways to cook your beans:

Slow-Cooked—A Crock-Pot makes this method simple because you don't have to watch the pot. As an alternative, a soup or stock pot with a lid can be used on the stove-top. Cooking time for this method is between 3 and 6 hours.

Fast Method—A pressure cooker speeds the cooking time. You need to make sure there is always water in the cooker. Cooking time for this method is between 45 and 90 minutes.

Speed Method—Grinding beans into a powder or flour will speed up the cooking time. You can grind beans in the blender or wheat grinder. Use one-fourth the amount of bean flour as the recipe calls for dry beans. Cooking time for this method is between 3 and 15 minutes.

Also, soaking beans overnight will cut cooking time in half. If you soak your beans you will need to adjust cooking times in the recipes.

BASIC COOKED BEANS

2 C. dry beans
1 tsp. vegetable oil (opt.)
1 tsp. garlic powder (opt.)
1 tsp. salt
1/4 tsp. pepper (opt.)
2 qts. water

Wash beans; remove all broken beans and any foreign objects. Place all ingredients in Crock-Pot. Cook on high 4-5 hours or until beans are tender.

You can cook any dry beans with this method. Check package directions for cooking times, as they may vary somewhat.

BEST REFRIED BEANS

2 C. dry pinto beans
1/2 tsp. chili powder
2 tsp. garlic powder
1 tsp. salt
2 qts. water
Cheese (opt.)

Sort (remove all broken beans and any foreign objects) and wash beans. Place all ingredients except cheese in Crock-Pot. Cook on high 4-5 hours. Mash beans or puree in blender.

Refried beans are most commonly used with Mexican dishes. For creamier beans, add 1/2 cup grated cheese when blending.

DELICIOUS BLACK BEANS

2 C. dry black beans
2 qts. water
1 onion, chopped
1 garlic clove, minced
1 Tbsp. vinegar

1 Tbsp. lemon juice
1 tsp. molasses (opt.)
1 Tbsp. beef bouillon
1 tsp. oregano
1/4 tsp. cayenne pepper

Sort (remove all broken pieces and any foreign objects) and wash beans. Place all ingredients in Crock-Pot. Cook on high 4-5 hours or low 6-8 hours. These beans can be made without the onion and garlic; substitute 2 tsp. garlic powder and 1 Tbsp. minced onion.

HAMHOCKS AND BEANS

1 hamhock with ham meat
2 C. dry small white beans
1/2 onion, chopped
2 tsp. garlic powder

1/4 tsp. pepper
1 tsp. salt
2 qts. water

Place all ingredients in Crock-Pot. Cook on high 4-5 hours. Remove hamhock from pot. Remove any ham still remaining on bone. Discard bone. Cut ham into small bite-size pieces and return to pot.

Beans may cause gas as they are digested because the enzyme needed to break down beans is not present in the average person's stomach. Soaking beans helps break them down, or you can purchase products such as "Beano" that have the enzyme needed. As you continue to eat beans in your diet, your body should naturally develop this enzyme.

BOSTON BAKED BEANS

2 C. dry navy beans
2 qts. water
1/4 lb. bacon, cut up
1 onion, chopped
1/2 C. molasses or maple syrup

1/4 C. brown sugar
1 tsp. dry mustard
1/2 tsp. salt
1/4 tsp. black pepper

Sort (remove all broken pieces and any foreign objects) and wash beans. Place beans and 2 qts. water in Crock-Pot. Cook on high 4-5 hours or until beans are tender. Drain beans, reserving liquid. Brown bacon. Add bacon, bacon drippings, 1 C. reserved bean liquid, and remaining ingredients to Crock-Pot. Cook on high, stirring occasionally, 1-2 hours or until desired thickness for sauce.

CREAMY NAVY BEAN CHOWDER

2 C. dry navy beans
2 qts. water
1 onion, chopped
2 carrots, shredded
1 Tbsp. chicken bouillon
2 tsp. garlic powder

1 tsp. salt
1/2 tsp. pepper
1/4 C. butter
1 10-oz. can
   evaporated milk

Sort (remove all broken pieces and any foreign objects) and wash beans. Place all ingredients except canned milk in Crock-Pot. Cook on high 4-5 hours. Mash beans slightly and add canned milk. Stir well and cook uncovered an additional 30 minutes or until thickened.

81

Soups and Stews

Using some of the basics from your food storage such as rice, corn, barley, and pastas, and combining them with fresh vegetables, herbs, and spices, you can make some delicious soups and stews. You can use bottled or dried vegetables if you don't have fresh vegetables. Also, some of the recipes in this section call for bottled meat. Refer to the Preserving Meats section if needed.

SWEET CARROT STEW

2 C. water
2 tsp. chicken bouillon
2 carrots, peeled and shredded
4 medium potatoes, chopped

1 medium onion, chopped
1/4 tsp. ground ginger
1 tsp. parsley flakes
1 10-oz. can evaporated milk

Dissolve bouillon in water in a soup pot. Place next five ingredients in pot in order. Simmer on medium-low heat until potatoes are tender (about 30 minutes). Mash lightly and stir in evaporated milk.

Tip: Carrots, potatoes, and onions can keep all winter if stored in a cool, dry area. Onions need to have air circulate around them; hang them in netting or a nylon stocking, tying knots between onions.

BEAN AND SAUSAGE STEW

1 lb. sweet Italian sausage
1 Tbsp. chicken bouillon
2 qts. water
2 carrots, peeled and chopped
1 stalk celery, chopped

1/2 C. dry pinto beans
1 C. dry navy beans
1/2 C. dry kidney beans
1 tsp. garlic powder
1 16-oz. can diced tomatoes

Cook sausage until browned. Place sausage and remaining ingredients except tomatoes in Crock-Pot. Sprinkle with salt and pepper. Cook on high 4-5 hours or low 6-7 hours, until beans are tender. Add tomatoes and cook additional 30 minutes. If desired, sprinkle with Parmesan cheese.

"I am suggesting that the time has come to get our houses in order."

President Gordon B. Hinckley

CROCK-POT CHILI BEANS

2 lbs. ground beef
Salt, pepper, and garlic powder to taste
1/2 onion, chopped
2 C. small red beans

1 pkg. chili seasoning mix
2 qts. water
1 can tomato sauce
1 C. salsa

Brown ground beef with salt, pepper, and garlic powder. Drain fat. Combine hamburger and remaining ingredients except tomato sauce and salsa in Crock-Pot. Cook on high 4-6 hours or until beans are tender. Add tomato sauce and salsa and cook additional 30 minutes. If desired, sprinkle with fresh onions and grated cheese.

RED LENTIL CHILI

2 lbs. ground beef
Salt, pepper, and garlic powder
2 C. dry red lentils
1/2 onion, chopped
1 pkg. chili seasoning mix

1 Tbsp. beef bouillon
2 Tbsp. apple cider vinegar
2 qts. water
1 qt. tomatoes

Brown ground beef with salt, pepper, and garlic powder. Drain fat.
Combine ground beef with remaining ingredients except tomatoes
in Crock-Pot. Cook on high 4-6 hours or until beans are tender.
Add tomatoes. Cook additional 30 minutes. If desired,
top with fresh onions and grated cheese.

SPLIT PEA SOUP

1 lb. dry green split peas
1 hamhock
1/2 C. minced onions
2 tsp. chicken bouillon
2 1/2 qts. water

Salt and pepper
1/2 C. dehydrated diced carrots
1/2 C. dehydrated diced celery
1 10-oz. can evaporated milk
2 Tbsp. butter (dried or fresh)

Combine split peas, hamhock, minced onions, bouillon, water, salt, and pepper in a large soup pot. Bring to a boil. Cover and simmer 1 hour, stirring frequently. Add carrots and celery and simmer additional hour or until tender. Remove hamhock; de-bone and chop ham. Return chopped ham to soup. Stir evaporated milk and butter into soup and heat through.

FRESH LENTIL SOUP

4 slices bacon, cut up
2 C. dry lentils
2 qts. water
2 Tbsp. parsley flakes
1/2 tsp. garlic powder

1 tsp. Italian seasoning
1/2 C. onion, chopped
1 carrot, peeled and chopped
2 Tbsp. apple cider vinegar
1 16-oz. can diced tomatoes

Cook bacon in Crock-Pot. Do not drain bacon fat. Place remaining ingredients except diced tomatoes in Crock-Pot. Cook on high 2-3 hours or until lentils are tender. Add diced tomatoes and cook additional 30 minutes.

LENTIL-BURGER SOUP

Follow Fresh Lentil Soup recipe, but add 1 1-lb. ground beef in place of bacon. Brown the ground beef in Crock-Pot or frying pan. Drain the fat. Add hamburger and other ingredients except diced tomatoes. Continue as directed. Serve with a dollop of sour cream and grated cheese on top.

85

CREAM OF CHICKEN SOUP

1 3/4 C. water
4 tsp. chicken bouillon or base

5 Tbsp. white bean flour
1/2 C. chopped chicken (opt.)

Bring water and bouillon to a boil in small saucepan. Stir in bean flour and beat until smooth and thickened. Reduce heat and cook 2 minutes more. Remove from heat. Pour mixture into blender. Blend on high 2 minutes. If desired, add 1/2 C. chopped chicken pieces. Use as a substitute for canned cream of chicken soup. May be stored in refrigerator up to one week.

CREAM OF MUSHROOM SOUP

Follow Cream of Chicken Soup recipe, but use 1 4-oz. can mushrooms (drained) in place of chopped chicken. Use as a substitute for canned cream of mushroom soup.

CREAM OF CELERY SOUP

Follow Cream of Chicken Soup recipe, but use 1/2 C. diced celery in place of chopped chicken. Use as a substitute for canned cream of celery soup.

GARDEN TOMATO SOUP

3 C. water
8 large garden tomatoes
1 onion, chopped
2 ribs celery, chopped
2 tsp. chicken bouillon

1 tsp. garlic powder
2 Tbsp. parsley flakes
Salt and pepper
1/4 cup butter
2 Tbsp. flour

Bring water and tomatoes to a boil in large pot.
Remove tomatoes from pot and remove skins. Return
to pot with remaining vegetables, bouillon, and seasonings. Simmer 20 minutes. Remove from heat. Pour 1/2 of mixture into blender. Blend on high until pureed. Repeat with remaining mixture. Melt butter in pan. Add flour and mix well. Slowly stir in tomato puree. Cook on medium heat, stirring constantly until soup thickens.
Note: You can also use bottled tomatoes for this recipe. Substitute 1 qt. tomatoes for the fresh tomatoes and 2 C. of the water. Simmer other vegetables, bouillon, and seasoning together for 20 minutes. Puree bottled tomatoes (with juice) with cooked vegetables. Continue as directed.

QUICK TOMATO SOUP

3 Tbsp. butter
3 Tbsp. flour

2 C. water
2 8-oz. cans tomato sauce

Melt butter in medium saucepan. Stir in flour and cook until bubbly. Slowly pour in water while continually stirring. Add tomato sauce and continue cooking and stirring until soup comes to a boil. Season with salt and pepper if desired.

CREAMY VEGETABLE SOUP

4 potatoes, peeled and chopped
3 medium carrots, thinly sliced
1 medium onion, chopped
1 tsp. chicken bouillon
3 Tbsp. butter

2 C. water
1 16-oz. can green beans
1 16-oz. can stewed tomatoes
1 can evaporated milk

Cook first 3 vegetables, bouillon, and butter in water until vegetables are tender. Drain juice from green beans and tomatoes and add to the cooked vegetables. Continue cooking over medium heat 5-7 minutes. Mash vegetables gently. Stir in milk and heat through.

VEGETABLE, BARLEY, AND RICE SOUP

Follow Creamy Vegetable Soup recipe, but add 1/2 C. long-grain white rice and 1/2 C. barley with vegetables. Substitute beef bouillon for chicken bouillon. After vegetables and barley are tender, add drained green beans and 1 qt. stewed tomatoes (with juice) instead of the canned milk.

Cooked beef or chicken chunks may be added to this soup if desired.

LENTIL AND RICE SOUP

2 qts. water
1 C. dry lentils
1/2 C. rice
2 tsp. chicken bouillon

1 tsp. salt
1/4 tsp. pepper
2 onions, sliced
1/4 C. vegetable oil

Place all ingredients except onions and oil in Crock-Pot. Turn to high and begin cooking. Meanwhile, saute onions in oil until lightly browned. Add sauteed onions to Crock-Pot and cook 2-3 hours or until lentils are tender.

But if ye are prepared ye shall not fear.   D&C 38:30

BEEF AND NOODLE SOUP

1 lb. ground beef
1 C. celery, finely diced
1 C. carrots, finely diced
1/2 C. onion, finely diced

2 qts. water
2 tsp. beef bouillon
3 C. egg noodles
Salt and pepper to taste

Brown beef in large soup pot. Drain excess fat. Add celery, carrots, and onion, and saute vegetables about 5 minutes. Add water and bouillon; cook 1 hour or until vegetables are tender. Add noodles and continue cooking until noodles are done. Stir in salt and pepper and heat through.

CHICKEN-VEGETABLE ALPHABET SOUP

1 qt. water
1 tsp. chicken bouillon
2 C. frozen mixed vegetables
1 qt. chicken chunks

1/4 tsp. thyme
1/4 tsp. salt
2 Tbsp. parsley flakes
1 C. alphabet pasta

In large saucepan, bring water and bouillon to a boil. Add vegetables and return to a boil. Add pasta, chicken, thyme, and parsley. Boil 7-9 minutes or until pasta and vegetables are tender. Sprinkle with salt and pepper.

VEGETABLE, BEEF, AND RICE STEW

1 qt. water
1 qt. beef chunks
1/4 C. onions, chopped
2 celery ribs, sliced
2 tsp. beef bouillon

1 tsp. garlic powder
1 1/2 C. brown rice
1 qt. stewed tomatoes
1 qt. whole-kernel corn
1 qt. green beans

Combine all ingredients in a large saucepan. Bring to a boil. Cover and reduce heat. Simmer about 1 hour or until rice is tender. *Note:* You can substitute barley for the rice in this soup, or simply add barley.

CHICKEN AND RICE SOUP

1 qt. water
6 carrots, peeled and sliced
1 onion, chopped
4 ribs celery, sliced

1 qt. chicken chunks
1 tsp. chicken bouillon
1 1/2 C. long-grain rice
1 Tbsp. parsley flakes

Cook vegetables in water in large soup pot until tender. Add remaining ingredients and bring to a boil. Reduce heat and simmer 20 minutes or until rice is done.

CHICKEN NOODLE SOUP

Follow Chicken and Rice Soup recipe but substitute 3 C. egg noodles for the rice. Don't add egg noodles until soup boils. Add noodles and continue boiling until egg noodles are barely tender.

Egg Noodles

Combine 3 Tbsp. dried egg powder, 2 Tbsp. powdered milk, and 2 tsp. salt. Add 1/2 C. water and 1 tsp. oil and whisk together. Stir in about 2 C. flour until a stiff dough forms. Cover and let rest 10 minutes. Roll out to 1/16 inch. Roll up dough loosely. Cut strips 1/4-inch wide. Unroll and cut strips into 2- to 3-inch pieces. Use immediately or dry overnight before storing.

EASY CORN CHOWDER

2 C. water
1 tsp. chicken bouillon
3 C. dried diced potatoes
1 qt. whole-kernel corn
1/4 C. bacon bits (opt.)
1 10-oz. can evaporated milk
1 tsp. salt
1/4 tsp. pepper

Place first 4 ingredients in soup pot. Cover and cook until potatoes are tender, about 20 minutes. Softly mash potatoes. Add remaining ingredients and cook 10 more minutes.

Dried corn can be substituted for bottled corn. Soak 1 1/4 C. dried corn in 4 C. water overnight. Follow recipe as directed.

CLAM CHOWDER

4 slices bacon, cut up
2 6 1/2-oz. cans minced clams
2 C. dried diced potatoes
1/4 C. dried diced onions
1/4 C. dried diced celery
Salt and pepper to taste
3 Tbsp. unbleached flour
2 10-oz. cans evaporated milk
1 tsp. Worcestershire sauce

Cook bacon in soup pot until crisp. Do not drain bacon fat. Drain clams, reserving liquid. Add enough water to make 4 C. liquid. Add liquid and vegetables to cooked bacon. Sprinkle with salt and pepper. Cover and simmer 20 minutes or until potatoes are tender. Blend flour and canned milk, stirring the milk in slowly to prevent lumps. Add flour mixture and clams to soup. Cook and stir over medium heat until thickened and bubbly. Stir in Worcestershire sauce.

HAM AND POTATO CHOWDER

2 C. water
4 potatoes, peeled and chopped
1 carrot, peeled and shredded
1/4 C. chicken gravy mix

1 C. sandwich ham, chopped
1 C. milk
1 C. sour cream
1 C. sharp cheese, grated

Place water, potatoes, and carrots in a soup pot. Sprinkle chicken gravy mix over vegetables. Cover and simmer until potatoes are tender (about 20 minutes). Mash potatoes slightly. Stir in remaining ingredients and heat through.

CAULIFLOWER SOUP

2 C. water
4 potatoes, peeled and chopped
1 carrot, peeled and shredded
2 C. cauliflower, chopped

1/4 C. chicken gravy mix
1 C. milk
1 C. sour cream
1 C. sharp cheese, grated

Place water, potatoes, carrots, and cauliflower in a soup pot. Sprinkle chicken gravy mix over vegetables. Cover and simmer until vegetables are tender (about 30 minutes). Mash vegetables slightly. Stir in remaining ingredients and heat through.

One reason we should start cooking with our storage now is that by using the foods we store, we will also be rotating them. Our food storage isn't meant to be placed on a shelf as an heirloom that will be handed down from one generation to the next, but it is meant to help us sustain life . . . *today!*

We have been counseled to store 300 pounds of grains per adult for a one year's supply. This may sound like a lot (and it is), but I know there is a reason that we have been given this counsel. We can let those bags of wheat sit on our shelves for years and years and years, or we can make good use of what is inside those bags today.

Personally, I am grateful for the counsel to store these grains, and I have loved learning how to use them to make delicious meals for my family.

It is an adjustment to use whole grains. I would suggest starting slowly. Add a little wheat flour to your recipes at first, then continue increasing the amounts as your family gets used to it.

Once you start using your food storage you will have a better idea of how often you need to replace these basic grains and other foods. You will gain experience as to how to cook and use them wisely, and you will begin to care more about the valuable *stock* that is stored in your basement or storage room.

I know the day will come when wheat will be more valuable than gold, and those who have stored it and know how to use it will feel as though they are richer than kings.

COOKING WITH WHOLE WHEAT AND OTHER GRAINS

Whole Wheat

Whole wheat is, without a doubt, the most important food in your storage. Inexpensive and easy to store, it will last for many years and provides the most important nutrients for a daily diet. It can easily be sprouted for greens or ground into flour to make breads and cereals. When the Martin and Willey Handcart companies were delayed on their journey to Salt Lake, the wheat flour was literally what preserved their lives.

If you are going to use wheat, it is essential to have a way to grind the wheat. You can grind wheat in a blender to make cracked wheat for cereal and to use in some recipes, but to get a fine flour, you will need a wheat grinder. (Wheat grinders are available at preparedness food stores and online.)

There are a variety of wheat grains available, but the recipes in this section call for hard red wheat unless otherwise specified. I also recommend storing vital wheat gluten and wheat germ, as they are also used in some of these recipes. Both of these ingredients are available in grocery stores.

HONEY WHEAT BREAD

1 Tbsp. yeast
1 1/2 C. warm water
1/4 C. vegetable oil
1/3 C. honey
5-6 C. whole-wheat flour
1 1/2 tsp. salt
1 tsp. vital wheat gluten

Dissolve yeast in warm water. Stir in oil and
honey and let rest for 2-3 minutes. Add 2 cups flour, salt, and wheat gluten. Beat at low speed with electric mixer for 1 minute, and then on high for 2 minutes. Stir in as much remaining flour as you can stir in by hand. Turn onto floured surface and knead 8-10 minutes, adding enough flour to make a moderately stiff dough. Place in greased bowl and cover. Let rise until double. Punch down dough. Divide dough and shape into 2 loaves. Place in greased loaf pans and cover. Let rise until double. Bake at 375 for 35-45 minutes or until crust is brown and has a hollow sound when thumped. Place pans on cooling rack for 10 minutes. Remove from pans and cool bread loaves on rack.

HONEY WHEAT SCONES

Follow Honey Wheat Bread recipe for bread dough. Allow dough to rise until double in size. Heat oil in large pot or skillet. Pinch off golf ball–size pieces of dough. Stretch dough into 4 to 5 inch circles. Fry on both sides until golden brown.

WHEAT AND HONEY DINNER ROLLS

1 Tbsp. yeast
1/2 C. warm water
1/3 C. honey
1/2 C. butter
1 C. milk

2 eggs
4-5 C. whole-wheat flour
1 tsp. salt
1 tsp. vital wheat gluten

Dissolve yeast in warm water. Add honey and let rest. Meanwhile melt butter. Add milk to melted butter. Cool slightly and add to yeast mixture. Stir in eggs, 2 C. flour, salt, and wheat gluten until well mixed. Stir in as much remaining flour as you can stir in by hand. Turn onto floured surface and knead 8-10 minutes, adding enough flour to make a soft dough. Place in greased bowl, cover, and let rise in a warm place until double. Punch down dough. Dough will be sticky. Use enough flour to make dough workable. Divide dough into quarters. Divide each quarter into six pieces. Shape pieces into rolls, and place pieces on greased sheet-cake pan. Cover with plastic wrap and let rise in warm area until double (about 30 minutes). Bake at 400 for 12-15 minutes or until golden brown. Place pan on cooling rack. Brush tops of rolls with butter.

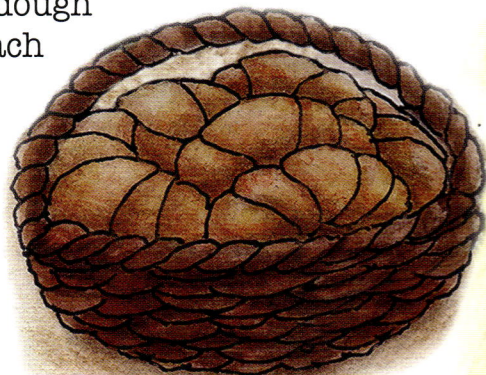

Honey is often used in wheat bread recipes because the honey acts as a preservative. Sugar may be substituted for honey, but if so, the bread must be eaten within a few days.

HEAVENLY SURPRISE DINNER ROLLS

1 Tbsp. yeast
1/2 C. warm water
1/2 C. sugar
1/2 C. butter
1 C. milk

2 eggs
3-4 C. unbleached flour
1 tsp. salt
3/4 C. cracked wheat

Dissolve yeast in warm water. Add sugar and let rest. Meanwhile, melt butter. Add milk to melted butter. Cool slightly and add to yeast mixture. Stir in eggs, 2 C. unbleached flour, salt, and cracked wheat until well mixed. Stir in as much remaining flour as you can stir in by hand. Turn onto floured surface and knead 8-10 minutes, adding enough flour to make a soft dough. Place in greased bowl and cover. Let rise in warm place until double. Punch down dough. Dough will be sticky. Use enough flour to make dough workable. Grease two 12-cup muffin tins. Roll dough out to 1/8-inch thickness. Spread butter over top and roll dough up cinnamon-roll style. Cut as you would for cinnamon rolls. Fold rolls into quarters and push into muffin cups. Cover with plastic wrap and let rise 30 minutes. Bake at 400 for 12-15 minutes or until golden brown. Place pan on cooling rack. Brush tops of rolls with butter. When cool enough to handle, remove rolls from muffin cups and place on cooling rack. (The surprise is the tasty bits of cracked wheat!)

These rolls are a great way to start putting a little wheat into the diet. They are soft and flaky and have just a hint of wheat.

SOURDOUGH STARTER

1 Tbsp. dry yeast	2 C. unbleached flour
2 C. warm water	1/4 C. sugar

Dissolve yeast in warm water in a 2-qt. canning jar or plastic container. Do not use metal. Let stand for 10 minutes. Stir in flour and sugar. Cover and let stand at room temperature until bubbly and sour (about 2 days). Use a portion for a recipe. Add to remaining starter: 1 C. flour, 1 C. milk, and 1/4 C. sugar. Store at room temperature, stirring it down every day and taking some from it each week for recipes.

SOURDOUGH BISCUITS

1 C. sourdough starter	1 tsp. salt
1 C. warm water	1/4 C. sugar
1/2 tsp. baking soda	4-5 C. unbleached flour
1/2 cup vegetable oil	

Combine first 4 ingredients in glass or plastic bowl. Add salt, sugar, and 2 C. of the flour. Stir until smooth. Continue adding flour and stirring until sides of bowl are clean. Turn onto floured surface and knead 6-8 minutes. Shape into 24 biscuits and place on greased baking sheet. Cover and let rise in warm place until double (about 1 hour). Bake at 350 for 15-20 minutes.

If you are running low on yeast, a sourdough starter will last indefinitely. Just add to your starter each time you take some from it. You can store the starter in the refrigerator to slow yeast growth. When removed from the refrigerator, the yeast will once again start to grow.

Some of the recipes call for *unbleached* flour. Whenever I use white flour I use unbleached flour. When making white flour, the wheat kernels are stripped before being ground into flour. Then, in order to get the flour white, they have to bleach it using chemicals. I think the bleaching makes the flour taste bland, so I use unbleached. But any white flour will work.

BUTTERMILK BISCUITS

2 C. unbleached flour
1 Tbsp. baking powder
1/2 tsp. baking soda
2 Tbsp. sugar

1 tsp. salt
1/4 C. buttermilk powder
1/2 C. shortening
2/3 C. water

Sift dry ingredients together in large bowl. Cut in shortening until mixture is coarse and crumbly. Mix in just enough water until dough forms. Turn onto lightly floured surface and roll to 3/4-inch thickness. Cut with biscuit cutter and place on ungreased baking sheet. Bake at 400 for 12-15 minutes or until lightly golden. Cool on wire rack.

WHOLE-WHEAT BISCUITS

You can substitute whole-wheat flour in both of the previous recipes. *Note:* Reduce water by 2 Tbsp. in each recipe. Wheat recipes call for less liquid than white flour recipes.

WHOLE-WHEAT BAGELS

1 pkg. (2 1/2 tsp.) yeast
1 1/2 C. warm water
1/4 C. brown sugar

4 1/2 C. whole-wheat flour
Baking soda

Combine yeast, warm water, and sugar. Let stand 5 minutes. Add flour and beat with dough hook until smooth, or knead on floured surface 6-7 minutes or until smooth. Let rest 5-10 minutes. Meanwhile, fill a saucepan 3/4 full with water. For every cup of water, add 2 tsp. baking soda. Bring water and soda to a boil. Divide dough into 12 pieces. Shape each piece into a flattened round disk. Press thumbs into center and pull dough outward to make a center hole. Drop each bagel in boiling water for about 10 seconds. Remove with a slotted spoon. Place bagels on greased baking sheet. Bake at 450 for 8-9 minutes or until browned.

SPROUTED-WHEAT BAGELS

Follow Whole-Wheat Bagels recipe, but add 1/4 C. new (less than 1/4-inch) wheat sprouts (see sprouting page in Preserving Foods section). Continue as directed.

"Five or six cans of wheat in the home are better than a bushel in the welfare granary."

President Gordon B. Hinckley

QUICK FRIED BREAD

2 C. wheat or white flour
4 tsp. baking powder
1 tsp. salt
1/2 to 3/4 C. water

Mix dry ingredients. Slowly stir in water until a nice dough forms. Pull off golf ball–size pieces and stretch into 5- to 6-inch circles. Fry bread in hot oil, turning to cook both sides. Place on paper towel to drain excess oil. Use for Navajo Tacos or as a treat with jam or honey spread on top.

WHOLE-WHEAT PITA BREAD

2 tsp. yeast
1 C. warm water

2 1/2 C. whole-wheat flour
1 tsp. salt

Dissolve yeast in warm water. Add flour and salt, and stir to make a soft dough. Knead well, adding a little flour if needed. Place in greased bowl. Cover and let rise 15 minutes. Divide dough into 8 balls. Cover and let rise 10 minutes. Flatten each ball and use rolling pin to roll into a thin circle (about 1/4-inch thick). Place on greased baking sheet. Bake at 500 for 4 to 6 minutes until puffed and lightly browned.

These pitas are perfect for chicken or turkey salad sandwiches. (See recipe in Preserving Meats section.)

103

WHITE-WHEAT CRISPY PIZZA CRUST

1 tsp. yeast
1 3/4 tsp. salt
1 3/4 C. cold water

4 1/2 C. white wheat flour
1/4 C. vegetable oil

Combine all ingredients and mix well. Place in greased bowl, cover, and refrigerate overnight. To make crust, divide dough into two balls. Stretch each ball into a 12-inch circle. Grease two pizza pans and sprinkle with cornmeal. Place dough on pans and top with sauce, cheese, and toppings. Bake at 450 for 10-12 minutes or until crust is crispy and golden brown.

RED-WHEAT PIZZA CRUST

2 1/2 tsp. yeast
1 1/4 C. warm water
1/4 C. vegetable oil

4-5 C. whole-wheat flour
1 1/2 tsp. salt

Dissolve yeast in warm water. Add vegetable oil, flour, and salt, and stir to make a soft dough. Knead well, adding a little flour if needed. Place in greased bowl. Cover and let rise 15 minutes. Divide dough into two balls. Stretch each ball into a 12-inch circle. Grease two pizza pans and sprinkle with cornmeal. Place dough on pans and top with sauce, cheese, and toppings. Bake at 450 15-20 minutes or until crust is well-browned on bottom and edges.

SOFT WHOLE-WHEAT BREADSTICKS

1 Tbsp. yeast
2 Tbsp. sugar
1 tsp. salt
3 1/2 C. whole-wheat flour
1 1/2 C. hot water

1/2 C. butter
Garlic salt
Italian seasoning
Parmesan cheese

Sift first 3 dry ingredients together with 2 C. of flour. Add hot water and beat until well blended. Mix in remaining flour. Place in greased bowl, cover, and let rise 15 minutes. Knead on lightly floured surface. Spread dough evenly on sheet-cake pan. Using a pizza cutter, cut lengthwise down center and then crosswise every 2 inches to make breadsticks. Spread melted butter over tops. Sprinkle with garlic salt, Italian seasoning, and Parmesan cheese. Bake at 375 for 20-25 minutes or until golden brown.

Note: This recipe is from my daughter-in-law. The breadsticks are great with pizza and also wonderful served with hot soups and chili.

The next time you want to order out for pizza, make a few homemade pizzas instead. You can buy one or two bags of wheat for your storage with the money saved.

SESAME WHOLE-WHEAT BREADSTICKS

2 C. unbleached white flour
2 C. whole-wheat flour
1 pkg. (2 1/2 tsp.) yeast
2 tsp. salt
1 tsp. sugar

2 C. lukewarm water
4 Tbsp. olive or vegetable oil
1 egg white, lightly beaten
Sesame seeds for sprinkling

Combine the flours, yeast, salt, and sugar in a bowl, and make a well in the center. Gradually stir in water and oil. Stir in additional flour, if necessary, to make a stiff dough. Turn onto lightly floured surface and knead 8-10 minutes until smooth and elastic. Place dough in greased bowl and cover tightly. Put in warm place and let rise until double. Turn dough onto lightly floured surface and knead lightly. Divide into 2 equal pieces. Roll each piece into a 16-inch rope, and then cut each rope into 1-inch pieces. Cover the dough you are not working with to prevent it from drying out. Roll each piece into a thin breadstick. Carefully transfer to greased baking sheet. Cover and set aside to rise for 10 minutes. Brush with egg white. Sprinkle evenly and thickly with sesame seeds. Bake at 450 for 10 minutes. Brush again with egg white and bake an additional 5 minutes or until golden brown and crisp. Cool on wire rack.

Learn to sustain yourselves;
lay up grain and flour and save it against a day of scarcity.

—Brigham Young

BROWN SUGAR MUFFINS

1/2 C. butter
1 C. brown sugar
2 eggs
1 tsp. soda
1/2 tsp. salt

1 C. milk
1 tsp. vanilla
2 C. whole-wheat flour
1/2 C. raisins (opt.)
1/2 C. walnuts (opt.)

Cream butter, brown sugar, and eggs together. If desired, chop raisins and walnuts and stir into creamed mixture. Add soda and salt and mix well. Stir in milk and vanilla. Add flour and stir until just moist. Pour into greased or paper-lined muffin cups. Bake at 375 for 20 minutes. Yield: 2 dozen muffins.

APPLESAUCE MUFFINS

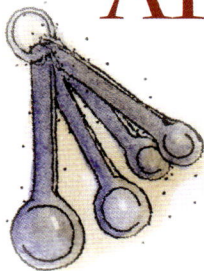

2 C. applesauce
1/2 C. butter, softened
1 C. sugar
2 eggs, well-beaten
2 C. whole-wheat flour

1 1/2 tsp. baking soda
1/2 tsp. salt
2 tsp. ground cinnamon
1 tsp. ground ginger
1 tsp. ground allspice

Mix first four ingredients until well blended. Sift dry ingredients together. Stir into applesauce mixture until just moist. Pour into greased or paper-lined muffin cups. Bake at 350 for 20 minutes or until tops are golden brown. Yield: 2 dozen muffins.

WHOLE-WHEAT PANCAKES

2 C. whole-wheat flour
4 tsp. baking powder
2 Tbsp. sugar
1 tsp. salt

1/4 C. powdered milk
2 eggs
1/4 C. vegetable oil
2 C. water

Mix dry ingredients together. Beat egg, oil, and water together until well blended. Pour into dry ingredients and stir just until moist. Drop onto hot oiled griddle. Cook until bubbles appear all over and edges are browned. Flip pancake over and cook other side. *Note:* This recipe is also very good using white-wheat flour.

BLENDER WHEAT PANCAKES

3/4 C. wheat
1 C. milk
1/4 C. butter
1 egg

2 Tbsp. sugar
1 tsp. salt
1/4 tsp. baking soda

Blend wheat in a blender to produce a coarse flour. Add milk, butter, and egg, and blend until well mixed. Add sugar, salt, and baking soda. Blend on high until mixed. Pour batter onto hot greased griddle. Cook until bubbles appear all over and edges start to brown. Flip and cook other side.

Maple Syrup: Stir 2 C. water and 1 C. sugar in saucepan. Boil 5-7 minutes until syrup thickens. Remove from heat and stir in 1 tsp. maple flavoring.

HEARTY WHEAT GERMAN PANCAKES

1/4 C. butter
6 eggs, well-beaten
1 C. milk

1 C. whole-wheat flour
1 tsp. salt

Place butter in 9 x 13 baking pan. Place pan in preheating oven to melt butter (don't let it burn). In a separate bowl, beat eggs. Add milk, flour, and salt, and mix well. Pour batter over melted butter. Bake at 450 for 15-20 minutes or until edges are golden brown. *Note:* This recipe is also very good using white-wheat flour.

WHITE-WHEAT FRENCH CREPES

1 C. white-wheat flour
1/2 tsp. salt
6 large eggs

2 1/2 C. milk
1 Tbsp. vanilla
1/2 C. butter, melted

Sift flour and salt together. In a separate bowl, whisk eggs, milk, vanilla, and melted butter together. Add to flour mixture and mix well. Heat and lightly butter or oil small skillet. Use a measuring cup to pour 1/4 C. batter into skillet. Quickly swirl pan to spread batter. Cook until edges are brown. Flip crepe and cook other side. Sprinkle with powdered sugar or flavored gelatin and roll up, or serve with fruit, meat, or vegetable fillings.

CRACKED-WHEAT CEREAL

2 C. water
3/4 C. cracked wheat

1/2 tsp. salt
1/3 C. sugar

Bring water to a boil in a saucepan. Add cracked wheat, salt, and sugar and stir well. Reduce heat and simmer about 5 minutes or until wheat is soft. Serve with milk, cream, or canned milk.

GRAPE-NUT CEREAL

1 1/2 C. whole-wheat flour
1/2 C. brown sugar
1/4 C. wheat germ
2 Tbsp. powdered milk

1 Tbsp. malted milk powder
1 Tbsp. baking powder
1/2 tsp. salt
1/2 C. water

Combine all ingredients. Spread dough (it will be sticky) on a greased sheet-cake pan. Bake at 350 for 20-25 minutes or until browned. Place pan on cooling rack and allow to cool. Break cereal into pieces and grind in meat grinder to get coarse crumbs. Place in warm oven to dry.

Homemade wheat, corn, and oat cereal costs about 5 to 10 cents per serving compared to 20 to 40 cents per serving for store-bought packaged cold cereals. That's not all: your family will usually eat two to three servings of those packaged cereals compared to one serving of homemade cereal. For a family of six that's a savings of $50 to $150 (or more) per month.

WHEAT FLAKES CEREAL

3/4 C. coarse-ground wheat flour
1 C. water

1 tsp. salt
2 Tbsp. sugar

Combine all ingredients and stir until there are no lumps. Pour half the batter onto greased sheet-cake pan. Tip pan back and forth until layer of batter is thin. Batter will be slightly uneven. Repeat with second sheet-cake pan. Bake both pans at 375 for 5 minutes. Remove from oven. Slide pancake turner under cooked batter to loosen from pan. (This is to prevent sticking. It will come up a little messy, but that is okay.) Return to oven. Cook additional 10-12 minutes or until edges start to brown. Cool slightly. Break cereal into flakes.

Raisin Bran: Add 1/2 C. wheat bran and 1/4 C. water to recipe. After cereal has been broken into flakes, add 1/4 C. raisins. Mix well.

CORN FLAKES CEREAL

3/4 C. cornmeal flour
1 Tbsp. cornstarch
2 Tbsp. malted milk powder
1 Tbsp. sugar

1 tsp. salt
1 Tbsp. sugar
2 Tbsp. honey
1/2 C. water

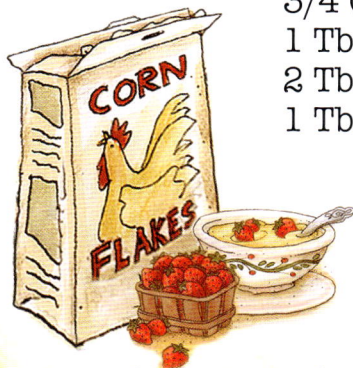

Grind cornmeal into flour. Sift dry ingredients together. Add honey and water and stir until well blended. Follow cooking directions for Wheat Flakes Cereal.

111

Dried Corn

I love the taste of corn! It has a sweet but hearty flavor and is perfect when you want a little variation from wheat. Look for more corn recipes in the Beans, Soups, and Stews section and the Main and Side Dishes section.

FRESH CORNBREAD

2 C. white-wheat flour
1 C. cornmeal
1 1/2 tsp. salt
1/4 C. sugar
1/3 C. powdered milk

4 Tbsp. baking powder
1/3 C. vegetable oil
3 eggs, well-beaten
1 1/2 C. water

Sift dry ingredients together. In a separate bowl, blend eggs, oil, and milk. Mix with dry ingredients just until moist. Pour into greased 9 x 13 baking pan. Bake at 425 for 20 minutes or until golden brown.

CORNMEAL MUFFINS

Follow Fresh Cornbread recipe, but pour batter into greased muffin cups. Bake at 400 for 12-15 minutes or until golden brown.

CORNMEAL MUSH

3 C. water

1 tsp. salt

1 1/2 C. cornmeal

1/3 C. honey or sugar

Bring water and salt to a boil. Gradually sprinkle in cornmeal, stirring constantly. Reduce heat and cook 4-5 minutes, stirring frequently, until mush thickens. Stir in honey or sugar. Serve with milk or cream.

"We suggest that members concentrate on essential foods that sustain life."

First Presidency Letter
June 24, 1988

CORN TORTILLAS

2 C. corn masa* flour

1 tsp. salt

1 1/3 C. warm water

Combine masa, salt, and water until dough forms a ball; add more masa or water as needed. Wet hands to handle dough. Divide dough into 12 balls. Roll or flatten balls between two pieces of waxed paper. Cook on hot ungreased skillet for about 1 minute or until lightly browned. Flip tortilla and cook 1 minute on opposite side.

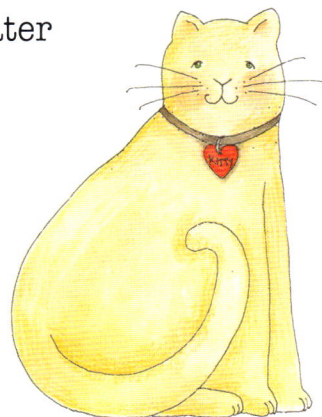

*You can buy corn masa in the grocery store where flour is sold, or you can make your own masa by using a wheat grinder to grind cornmeal into flour.

Rolled Oats

Although rolled oats are most commonly used to make oatmeal, there are many other uses for them. They can be used in breads and cereals, added to meat and side dishes, and they are one of my favorite ingredients in cookies and snacks. Following are a few recipes using rolled oats; for more recipes, see the Snacks and Treats section.

STOVE-TOP GRANOLA

1/3 C. butter
1/3 C. granulated sugar
1/3 C. brown sugar
1/3 C. honey
1/3 C. milk

1/3 C. peanut butter
1 tsp. vanilla
3-4 C. quick oats
3/4 C. raisins (opt.)
1/2 C. coconut (opt.)

Melt butter in medium saucepan. Stir in next 4 ingredients. Cook and stir over medium heat until mixture starts to boil. Boil for 1 minute. Remove from heat and stir in peanut butter, vanilla, oats, and, if desired, raisins and coconut. Cool completely before using as granola. My kids like to eat it soft, as it is in this recipe. For crispy granola, follow directions in Oven-Toasted Granola.

OVEN-TOASTED GRANOLA

Spread Stove-Top Granola on a large cookie sheet. Broil for 3-4 minutes (watch closely) or until lightly toasted on top. Turn mixture; broil again (watch closely) until lightly toasted on top. Remove from oven and cool.

NATURAL GRANOLA

1/3 C. vegetable oil
1/2 C. honey
1/4 C. brown sugar
1/2 tsp. salt

1/2 C. wheat germ
2 tsp. vanilla
3-4 C. quick-
    cooking oats

Mix all ingredients. Spread on sheet-cake pan and bake at 350 for 10 minutes. Stir and bake 10 minutes longer. Stir again. Continue baking and stirring until golden brown. Cool completely.

FRUIT AND NUT GRANOLA

Follow recipe for Natural Granola. After toasting 10 minutes, stir in 1/2 C. raisins or other dried fruit and 1/2 C. sliced almonds. Return to oven and continue toasting as directed.

OATMEAL MUFFINS

2 eggs, well-beaten
1 C. milk
1/2 C. vegetable oil
1 1/2 C. sugar

4 tsp. baking powder
1/2 tsp. salt
1 C. rolled oats
2 C. flour

Mix eggs, milk, and oil until well-blended. Sift dry ingredients together. Stir into wet mixture until just moist. Fill greased or paper-lined muffin cups 1/2 full. Bake at 400 for 15 minutes or until tops are golden brown.

OATMEAL BREAD

2 tsp. yeast
1 1/2 C. warm water
2 Tbsp. vegetable oil
2 Tbsp. honey

3 1/2 C. whole-
    wheat flour
1 1/2 tsp. salt
2/3 C. rolled oats

Dissolve yeast in warm water. Stir in oil and honey and let rest for 2-3 minutes. Add 2 cups flour, salt, and oats. Beat at low speed with electric mixer for 1 minute, and then on high for 2 minutes. Stir in as much remaining flour as you can stir in by hand. Turn onto floured surface and knead 8-10 minutes, adding enough flour to make a moderately stiff dough. Place in greased bowl and cover. Let rise until double. Punch down dough. Place in greased loaf pan and cover. Let rise until double. Bake at 375 for 35-45 minutes or until crust is browned. Place on cooling rack for 10 minutes. Remove from loaf pan and cool completely on rack.

HOT OATMEAL

2 C. water
1 C. quick oats

1/2 tsp. salt
1/4 C. sugar

Bring water to a boil. Add remaining ingredients and reduce heat. Simmer and stir until oatmeal thickens. Serve with milk or cream.

BROWN SUGAR OATMEAL

2 C. water
1 C. quick oats
1/2 tsp. salt

2 Tbsp. butter
1/3 C. brown sugar
1/4 C. raisins

Boil water. Add remaining ingredients and reduce heat. Simmer and stir until sugar dissolves and oatmeal thickens. Serve with milk or cream.

INSTANT-OATS PACKETS

1/4 C. quick oats
1/8 tsp. salt

2 Tbsp. oatmeal flour*
1 Tbsp. sugar

Combine ingredients in small zip-top bags. *To make oatmeal flour, grind oats in blender.

For other varieties, add ingredients to the packets as follows:
Cinnamon Raisin: 1/4 tsp. cinnamon and 2 Tbsp. raisins
Strawberries 'n Cream: 2 Tbsp. dried strawberry pieces

To prepare: Empty packet into microwave-safe bowl. Add 2/3 C. water and microwave on high 60-90 seconds. Stir and serve with milk or cream.

117

Rice

Rice is one of the most commonly used grains. I use it as an ingredient in soups, main dishes, and also serve it plain with meals. Look for more rice recipes in the Main and Side Dishes section.

BASIC COOKED RICE

4 C. water
2 C. white rice

2 Tbsp. butter (opt.)
1 tsp. salt

Bring water to a boil. Add remaining ingredients and reduce heat to medium-low. Cover with a tight-fitting lid and simmer 20 minutes or until rice is tender. Remove from heat, fluff with a fork, and replace lid until ready to serve.

COOKED BROWN RICE

Follow Basic Cooked Rice directions, but increase cooking time to 35-40 minutes or until rice is tender. You also may need to increase water.

BAKED RICE PUDDING

4 Tbsp. dried egg powder
2 cans evaporated milk
1/2 C. water
1/2 C. sugar

1 1/2 tsp. vanilla
2 tsp. cinnamon
2 C. cooked rice
3/4 C. raisins

Combine egg powder, milk, water, sugar, vanilla, and cinnamon in a 9 x 13 baking pan. Fold in rice and raisins. Bake at 350 for 20 minutes. Stir pudding and bake additional 20 minutes or until firm.

SLOW-COOKED RICE PUDDING

Follow Baked Rice Pudding recipe, but place ingredients in Crock-Pot. Cook on low for 2-3 hours or until pudding is firm.

Brown rice has more nutrients than white rice, but because there is oil in the outer shell of the grain it can go rancid rapidly. Store in the freezer for best results. White rice doesn't have as many nutrients but it is a good filler and has a shelf life of 30 or more years.

Did you know that you can make tasty fudge and pecan pie with pinto beans? Is it hard to imagine that with honey, wheat, and powdered milk you can make yummy cookies, cakes, and candies like mints, chewy caramels, and even tootsie rolls?

You can make these and many other snacks and treats with basic food storage items that may already be stocked on your shelves.

If you are faced with a crisis or challenge and your family has to rely on your food storage, having fresh and tasty treats and snacks will make the situation so much more enjoyable, and enduring the trial will be all the easier.

Even if you never have to rely on your food storage, you'll want to make these homemade snacks and treats. They are better for your health (no preservatives or hydrogenated fats), and they are far less expensive than the commercial snacks and treats available in the stores.

Recipes for fruit leather and dried fruit snacks are in the Growing and Preserving for a Rainy Day section.

These are the foods I find the most fun—they are like the icing on the cake! That's why I saved this section for last. You will want to make these treats over and over. So whenever you're in the mood for a salty or sweet treat, you won't have to go very far. I hope you and your family will enjoy these snacks and treats made from basic items found on your food storage shelves.

SNACKS
AND
TREATS

Savory Snacks

TASTY WHEAT NUTS

1 C. whole wheat
1/2 tsp. salt

3 C. water
3 Tbsp. cooking oil

Boil wheat and salt in 3 C. water until wheat skins puff up and soften. Drain and pat dry on paper towel. Heat oil in a skillet. Add wheat and stir-fry until wheat stops sizzling and kernels are browned. Dump popped wheat nuts onto paper towels and sprinkle with salt. Cool before eating.

Variations: Sprinkle with ranch dressing mix, barbecue seasoning, or other seasonings.

ROASTED CORN NUTS

1 C. dried whole-kernel corn
1/2 tsp. salt

3 C. water
3 Tbsp. cooking oil

Boil corn and salt in 3 cups water until corn begins to puff and soften. Spread corn on a sheet-cake pan. Sprinkle with salt or seasoning. Bake at 400 for 30-40 minutes. Cool 20 minutes before eating.

Variations: Sprinkle with ranch dressing mix, barbecue seasoning, or other seasonings.

GARLIC BAGEL CHIPS

4-6 wheat bagels
1/4 C. bottled butter

1/2 tsp. garlic powder
1/4 tsp. salt

Cut bagels into 1/4-inch thick slices. Place on a sheet-cake pan. Mix butter or oil with garlic powder and salt. Brush bagel chips with garlic butter. . Bake at 150 for 1 1/2 - 2 hours or until crisp and dry.

Spicy-Hot Bagel Chips: Add 1/4 tsp. cayenne pepper and 2 tsp. hot sauce to butter recipe. Continue as directed.

Zesty Bagel Chips: Decrease garlic powder to 1/4 tsp. and add 2 tsp. Worcestershire sauce to butter recipe. Continue as directed.

CHEESY POPCORN

1 C. popping corn
3 Tbsp. bottled butter

2 Tbsp. cheddar
cheese sauce powder

Pop corn in hot-air popper. Melt butter and pour over popcorn. Sprinkle powdered cheese over and mix well.

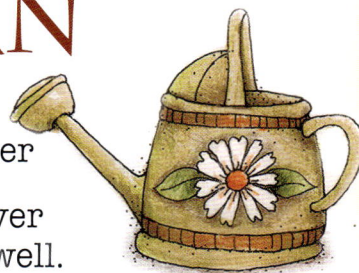

Bottled Butter:

Melt 2 lbs. butter in saucepan. (Use 1 lb. unsalted and 1 lb. salted, or the butter will be too salty.) As butter cools, skim the milk off the top. (Don't discard; you can use this in any recipe that calls for milk.) Pour remaining butter into a 1-qt. jar. Place lid and ring on the jar, and it is ready to store. Bottled butter tastes more like an oil, but it works for baking and it's great for popcorn. Bottled butter will store 6-9 months.

TORTILLA CHIPS

12 corn tortillas   Cooking oil   Salt

Using a pizza cutter, cut tortillas into 6 wedges as
you would a pizza or pie. Heat oil in large skillet. Place a
few tortilla pieces in hot oil. Turn quickly. Using slotted spoon,
remove from oil as soon as they start to turn a golden color.
Place on paper towels and blot off oil. Sprinkle with salt.
Serve with Fresh Garden Salsa.

FRESH GARDEN SALSA

8-10 Roma tomatoes, finely diced
1/2 tsp. garlic powder
1 small jalapeno pepper
1/4 C. red onion, finely diced

1/4 C. white onion, finely diced
1/2 C. green pepper, finely diced
1/4 C. cilantro, chopped
Salt and pepper to taste

Place tomatoes in a medium glass bowl and mix in the garlic powder.
Meanwhile, heat a small skillet over medium heat. Roll pepper around in
hot skillet to slightly scorch skin. Carefully cut pepper open and remove
seeds. Chop pepper and add to tomatoes. Add remaining ingredients and
mix well. *Note:* You can use any tomatoes with this recipe, but Roma tomatoes don't leak as much juice as other tomatoes.

SESAME WHOLE-WHEAT CRACKERS

1 C. whole-wheat flour
1/4 C. oil
1/2 tsp. salt

4 Tbsp. sesame seeds
4 Tbsp. wheat germ
1/3 C. cold water

Mix all ingredients until well-blended. Roll out on lightly floured surface to about 1/8-inch thickness. Loosely roll up dough and unroll on greased sheet-cake pan. Sprinkle with salt. Using a pizza cutter, cut dough into small squares. Prick tops with fork tines. Bake at 400 for 12 minutes or until golden brown. Cool about 10 minutes. Remove crackers from pan.

THIN WHEAT CRACKERS

3/4 C. unbleached flour
1/4 C. whole-wheat flour
1/8 tsp. baking soda
1/2 tsp. salt

1/2 C. wheat germ
2 Tbsp. malted milk powder
3 Tbsp. oil
6-8 Tbsp. cold water

Sift dry ingredients together. Stir in oil until crumbly. Stir in enough water to make a firm dough. Roll dough out very thin on a greased and lightly floured sheet-cake pan. (When rolling, sprinkle flour on top of dough to prevent sticking.) Using a pizza cutter, cut dough into small squares. Sprinkle with salt. Prick tops with fork tines. Bake at 350 for 15 minutes or until golden brown. Cool about 10 minutes. Remove crackers from pan.

CHEESE-CRISP CRACKERS

1 1/4 C. whole-wheat or white flour
1/8 tsp. baking soda
1/4 tsp. salt

1/4 C. cheese powder
3 Tbsp. oil
6-8 Tbsp. cold water

Sift dry ingredients together. Stir in oil until crumbly. Stir in enough water to make a firm dough. Roll dough out very thin on a greased and lightly floured sheet-cake pan. (When rolling, sprinkle flour on top of dough to prevent sticking.) Using a pizza cutter, cut dough into small squares. Prick tops with fork tines. Sprinkle with salt. Bake at 350 for 15 minutes or until golden brown. Cool 10 minutes. Remove crackers from pan.

HONEY GRAHAMS

1 1/2 C. whole wheat flour
1/4 C. sugar
1/8 tsp. baking soda
1/2 tsp. salt

1/4 cup malted milk powder
2 Tbsp. honey
1/4 C. oil
6-8 Tbsp. cold water

Sift dry ingredients together. Stir in oil until crumbly. Stir in enough water to make a firm dough. If needed, knead in enough flour to make a workable dough. Roll dough to about 1/8-inch thickness. Using a pizza cutter, cut dough into squares. Prick tops with fork tines. Place on ungreased baking sheet. (If desired, roll dough on baking sheet.) Bake at 350 for 15-20 minutes or until golden brown. Cool about 10 minutes. Remove crackers from pan.

Sweet Treats

TOFFEE-HONEY GRAHAMS

9-12 graham crackers
1 C. sugar

3/4 C. evaporated milk
Walnuts, chopped (opt.)

Cover sheet-cake pan with graham crackers (homemade or store-bought). If desired, sprinkle with chopped walnuts. Combine sugar and canned milk in medium saucepan. Cook and stir over medium heat until mixture comes to a boil. Boil 30 seconds. Pour mixture over crackers. Bake at 350 for 5 minutes. Cool and cut apart.

"Yes, we are laying up resources in store, but perhaps the greater good is contained in the lessons of life we learn as we live providently and extend to our children their pioneer heritage."

President Spencer W. Kimball

PIONEER HONEY CANDY

2 C. honey   1 10-oz. can evaporated milk   1 C. sugar

Combine ingredients in a heavy saucepan. Cook and stir over medium-high
heat until mixture comes to hard-ball
stage. Pour onto buttered pan. When
cool enough to handle, pull like taffy
until golden. Roll into a fat rope. Place
on cookie sheet and cut into 1-inch
lengths.

HONEY-LEMON CANDY

Follow recipe for Pioneer Honey Candy, but reduce milk to 1/2 C. and
omit the sugar. Add 1/2 C. lemon juice after mixture is removed from
heat. Stir well. Continue as directed.

Note: These are really soothing for a sore throat.

BUTTERSCOTCH HONEYS

Follow recipe for Pioneer Honey Candy, but add 1 tsp. butterscotch flavoring
after mixture is removed from heat. Stir well. Continue as directed.

HONEY-BUTTER MINTS

2 Tbsp. honey
1 Tbsp. water
2 tsp. peppermint oil

2 Tbsp. butter
1 1/4 C. powdered sugar
Food coloring (opt.)

Combine honey and water together in a small saucepan. Cook and stir over medium heat until mixture comes to a boil. Boil until mixture starts to thicken. Remove immediately. Stir in peppermint oil, butter, and food coloring if desired. Fold in enough powdered sugar to make a stiff dough. Continue to knead in remaining powdered sugar. Roll dough into a rope. Place on cookie sheet and cut into 1/2-inch pieces. Allow to dry out.

MINT CHOCOLATES

Follow recipe for Honey-Butter Mints, but knead 1/4 C. cocoa in with the powdered sugar. Do not add food coloring.

OLD-FASHIONED TAFFY

2 C. white sugar   1/2 C. water   1/2 C. vinegar

Combine ingredients in a heavy saucepan. Cook and stir over medium-high heat until mixture comes to hard-ball stage. (Drop a tiny amount in very cold water. Mixture should form a hard ball.) Pour onto buttered cookie sheet. When cool enough to handle, pull taffy until no longer glossy. Cut into bite-size pieces, and wrap pieces in waxed paper.

HONEY CARAMELS

2 C. honey
1 12-oz. can evaporated milk
1 tsp. vanilla

3 Tbsp. butter
Nuts, chopped (opt.)

Combine honey and milk in a saucepan. Cook and stir over medium heat until mixture comes to a boil. Continue cooking, stirring occasionally, until mixture comes to firm-ball stage. Remove immediately. Stir in vanilla, butter, and chopped nuts if desired. Pour onto buttered pan. Cool and cut into squares. Wrap in waxed paper.

HONEY TOOTSIE ROLLS

1 C. honey
1 tsp. vanilla

1 C. non-instant dry milk
1/2 C. cocoa

Cook honey over medium-high heat until it reaches hard-ball stage. Remove from heat. Stir in vanilla. Combine dry milk and cocoa together and stir into honey mixture. When cool enough to handle, pull like taffy until no longer glossy. Roll into a rope. Place on cookie sheet and cut into 1-inch lengths.

PEANUT-HONEY BITES

Follow recipe for Honey Tootsie Rolls, but add 1/4 C. peanut butter and replace 1/2 C. cocoa with 1/2 C. powdered sugar.

PINTO BEAN FUDGE

1 C. pinto beans, cooked
1/4 C. milk
1/4 C. butter

1/2 C. cocoa powder
2 tsp. vanilla
2 C. powdered sugar

In a blender, puree cooked beans and milk until creamy. Melt butter in a small saucepan. Stir in cocoa until well blended. Add whipped beans and vanilla and stir. Gradually stir in enough powdered sugar to make a thick, creamy mixture. Spread in a buttered pan. Chill 1-2 hours.

PLAIN YOGURT

4 C. 2% low-fat milk
3 Tbsp. yogurt start*

1/2 C. instant dry milk

Mix 2% milk and dry milk in a 2-quart saucepan until dry milk is dissolved. Heat over low heat. Remove from heat and cool to 110 degrees. Remove skin from milk. Stir yogurt start until creamy. Add to warm milk and stir well. Pour into 2-quart glass baking dish. Cover with towel and place in 110-degree oven for 3-6 hours or until yogurt sets. Refrigerate until ready to use. Makes 1 quart.

Fruit Yogurt—At serving time, mix with fresh or frozen fruit or fruit jam.

*Yogurt start can be any plain yogurt you buy in the grocery store (as long as it contains active live cultures; check the label). You can also buy powdered yogurt culture from a health-food store; follow package directions.

WHOLE-WHEAT PIE CRUST

1 1/3 C. whole-wheat flour
1 1/3 C. unbleached flour
1 tsp. salt

3/4 C. shortening
6 Tbsp. cold water

Sift flours and salt together. Cut in shortening until coarse and crumbly. Sprinkle in water a few tablespoons at a time. Blend together with fork until dough forms into a ball. Roll out on lightly floured surface. Gently roll dough around rolling pin and lift over pie pan. Unroll dough and gently press down into sides and bottom of pan. Trim crust 1/2-inch wider than pan. Fold edge under and pinch to flute. Bake according to pie directions. Makes 1 9-inch double-crust or 2 9-inch single-crust pie shells.

Tip: For a tender flaky crust, fluff the flour with a whisk before you measure it into the mixing bowl. Use cold shortening or butter and cold water. Work the dough as little as possible so the dough will not get tough.

DUTCH APPLE PIE

1 prepared pie crust
2 C. dried apple slices
3 C. water
2/3 C. sugar
1/2 tsp. cinnamon

1/2 C. whole-wheat flour
1/2 C. enriched flour
1/2 C. butter
1/2 C. sugar

Prepare pie crust. Combine next 4 ingredients in a medium saucepan. Bring to a boil. Boil 1 minute. Pour into prepared crust. Combine remaining ingredients. Sprinkle over apple mixture. Bake at 375 for 35-40 minutes or until topping is browned.

BAKED PEACH COBBLER

1 biscuit recipe*
2 C. dried peach slices
4 C. water
2 C. sugar

1/4 C. lemon juice
1/2 C. cornstarch
1/2 tsp. nutmeg
1/4 tsp. cinnamon

*Prepare biscuit dough according to Buttermilk Biscuit recipe from Cooking with Whole Wheat and Other Grains section. Combine remaining ingredients in a medium saucepan. Bring to a boil. Boil 1 minute. Pour into 9 x 13 baking pan. Spread biscuit dough over peach mixture. Bake at 400 for 35-40 minutes or until biscuit topping is browned.

Whipped Topping: Using electric mixer, whip 1 C. chilled evaporated milk, 2 Tbsp. lemon juice, and 1/4 C. powdered sugar until stiff.

LEMONADE CREAM PIE

1 1/2 C. sugar
1/3 C. cornstarch
1/3 C. powdered milk
1 pkg. lemonade punch powder

2 C. water
2 Tbsp. lemon juice
Pinch of salt

Blend first 4 ingredients in a medium saucepan. Add water, lemon juice, and salt, and stir until dry ingredients are dissolved. Bring mixture to a boil. Continue cooking over medium-high heat, stirring continuously until thickened (7-10 minutes). Pour into baked pie crust; chill.

PINTO BEAN PECAN PIE

1 pie shell, unbaked
1/2 C. granulated sugar
1 C. brown sugar
2 eggs, beaten

1/2 C. butter, softened
1 C. pinto beans, cooked
1/4 C. milk
1/2 C. pecans, chopped

Cream sugars, eggs, and butter together until creamy. Puree beans in blender until smooth; stir into creamed butter mixture. Pour into unbaked pie shell. Top with pecans. Bake at 375 for 20 minutes. Reduce heat to 350 and bake an additional 25 minutes. Cool on wire rack before serving.

Note: This recipe can also be made without the pecans. Also, if desired, other nuts may be substituted for the pecans.

CINNAMON-SUGAR CRUSTS

Pie crust (leftover scraps)
1 Tbsp. butter, softened

1/2 C. sugar
1 tsp. cinnamon

Spread leftover pie crust scraps on an ungreased cookie sheet. Spread crust pieces with softened butter. Combine sugar and cinnamon and sprinkle over crust pieces. Bake at 425 for 10-15 minutes or until golden brown.

CARAMEL BREAD PUDDING

1 C. brown sugar
1/2 C. granulated sugar
2 Tbsp. butter
1 tsp. vanilla

1 12-oz. can evaporated milk
1 1/2 C. water
6 Tbsp. dried egg powder
4-5 slices dry bread, broken

Combine first five ingredients in a medium saucepan. Bring to a boil. Boil for 5 minutes. Remove from heat. Meanwhile, whisk water and egg powder together. Spread broken bread pieces in a casserole or baking dish. Pour water-egg mixture over bread. Bake at 350 for 30 minutes. Pour boiled sauce over bread and cook an additional 30 minutes or until firm.

Cinnamon-Raisin Bread Pudding: Add 1 tsp. ground cinnamon and 1/2 tsp. ground nutmeg to the dried eggs before blending with water. Stir 1/2 C. raisins into boiled mixture before pouring over bread pudding.

CHOCOLATE SNACK CAKE

1 2/3 C. wheat or white flour
1 C. brown or white sugar
1/4 C. cocoa
1 tsp. baking soda
1/2 tsp. salt

1 C. water
1/3 C. vegetable oil
1 tsp. vinegar
1/2 tsp. vanilla

Combine all ingredients. Pour into a greased 9 x 13 baking pan. Bake at 350 for 30-35 minutes or until knife inserted in center comes out clean.

BOTTLED-FRUIT CAKE

2 C. sugar
3/4 C. vegetable oil
1 qt. bottled fruit, undrained
4 C. wheat or white flour
4 tsp. baking soda

1 tsp. salt
1 tsp. nutmeg
1 Tbsp. cinnamon
1 tsp. ground cloves
Raisins, nuts (opt.)

Cream oil and sugar together in a large mixing bowl. Stir in fruit and juice; add raisins and nuts if desired. In a separate bowl, sift dry ingredients together. Stir into creamed mixture. Pour into greased 9 x 13 cake pan. Bake at 350 for 35-40 minutes or until knife inserted in center comes out clean.

This recipe can be made with any bottled or canned fruit.

CHOCOLATE-CHIP APPLESAUCE CAKE

1/2 C. vegetable oil
1 C. sugar
1/2-1 C. brown sugar
1 1/2 C. applesauce
2 1/2 C. wheat or white flour
1 tsp. cinnamon
1 tsp. allspice

1 tsp. baking powder
2 tsp. baking soda
1/4 tsp. salt
Brown sugar for topping
2 C. chocolate chips
1 C. raisins (opt.)
1 C. nuts, chopped (opt.)

Cream oil and sugars together in a large mixing bowl. Stir in applesauce, and raisins and nuts (if desired). In a separate bowl, sift dry ingredients together. Stir into creamed mixture. Pour into greased 9 x 13 cake pan. Sprinkle with brown sugar and 2 C. chocolate chips. Bake at 350 for 30 minutes.

These three cake recipes are great for food storage because they don't call for eggs. If a recipe calls for eggs and you don't have any, use one of these substitutes.

Egg Substitutions — Equivalent to one egg

1 heaping Tbsp. flaxseed meal + 1/4 C. cold water (beat 2-3 minutes)

1 tsp. unflavored gelatin + 3 Tbsp. cold water + 2 1/2 Tbsp. boiling water

1 Tbsp. mayonnaise

1 Tbsp. dehydrated eggs + 2 Tbsp. cold water

WHOLE-WHEAT ZUCCHINI BREAD

1 C. vegetable oil
3 C. zucchini, chopped
3 eggs
1 tsp. vanilla
2 C. sugar

3 C. flour
1 1/2 tsp. baking soda
1 tsp. salt
1 Tbsp. cinnamon

Blend oil and zucchini in blender until pureed. Add egg and vanilla and blend well. Sift dry ingredients together in a mixing bowl. Pour zucchini mixture into dry ingredients and stir well. Pour into greased loaf pans. Bake at 350 for 30-35 minutes or until a knife inserted in center comes out clean.

Whole-Wheat Zucchini Cake—Follow recipe, but pour batter into a greased 9 x 13 baking pan. Bake at 350 25-30 minutes or until a knife inserted in center comes out clean.

Chocolate Zucchini Cake—Follow recipe for Whole-Wheat Zucchini Cake, but add 1/3 C. cocoa to dry ingredients. Pour batter onto greased sheet-cake pan. Bake as directed. Spread chocolate icing over cake while warm.

Icing—Melt 1/4 C. butter in a small saucepan. Add 3 Tbsp. cocoa powder and 3 Tbsp. buttermilk. Bring to a boil. Remove from heat and stir in 2 1/4 C. powdered sugar and 1/2 tsp. vanilla. Beat until smooth. Add 3/4 C. chopped walnuts if desired. Spread quickly over warm sheet cake.

APPLES-N-BEANS CAKE

1 C. cooked pinto beans, mashed
1 C. sugar or 1/2 C. honey
1/4 C. vegetable oil
1 egg or 1 Tbsp. dried egg powder
1/2 tsp. cinnamon

1/2 tsp. allspice
2 C. whole-wheat flour
2 C. applesauce
2 tsp. vanilla
1/2 C. nuts, chopped

Cream mashed beans, sugar or honey, oil, and egg in a large mixing bowl. In a separate bowl, sift dry ingredients together. Stir into creamed mixture. Stir in applesauce, vanilla, and chopped nuts. Pour batter into a greased 9 x 13 baking pan. Bake at 375 30-40 minutes or until a knife inserted in center comes out clean.

BUTTERMILK SPICE CAKE

1 1/3 C. butter
1 1/2 C. sugar
1 tsp. vanilla
1 C. water
2 Tbsp. dried egg powder
1/4 C. buttermilk powder

3 C. flour
1 tsp. soda
1 tsp. salt
2 tsp. cinnamon
1 tsp. nutmeg

Cream first 3 ingredients. Stir in water. In a separate bowl, sift dry ingredients together. Mix dry ingredients with creamed mixture. Pour batter into a greased 9x13 baking pan. Bake at 350 for 30 minutes or until toothpick inserted in center comes out clean.

CHOCOLATE-CHIP APPLESAUCE COOKIES

1/4 C. vegetable oil
3/4 C. brown sugar
3/4 C. granulated sugar
3 C. whole-wheat flour
1/2 tsp. salt

2 eggs or 2 Tbsp. dried eggs
1 tsp. baking soda
3/4 C. applesauce
1 tsp. vanilla
1 12-oz. bag chocolate chips

Cream oil and sugars in a large mixing bowl. In a separate bowl, sift dry ingredients together. Stir into creamed sugar. Stir in applesauce, vanilla, and chocolate chips. Drop by spoonfuls onto a cookie sheet lined with waxed paper. Bake at 350 for 10-12 minutes or until firm and bottoms are brown. Cool on wire rack.

CHOCOLATE-CHIP PEANUT BUTTER BARS

Follow Chocolate-Chip Applesauce Cookies recipe, but replace whole-wheat flour with 2 1/2 C. white flour. Replace applesauce with peanut butter. Spread cookie dough in greased 12 x 15 sheet-cake pan. Bake at 350 for 20 minutes or until edges start to brown. Place pan on wire rack to cool. Cut into bars.

LUNCH-BOX COOKIES

1 C. rolled oats	1 Tbsp. honey
1 C. coconut	1/2 C. butter
1 C. flour	1 1/2 tsp. baking soda
1 C. sugar	2 Tbsp. boiling water

Sift dry ingredients together. Mix honey and butter together in saucepan. Cook and stir over medium heat just until butter melts. Stir baking soda into boiling water. Stir soda water into honey-butter mixture. Combine with dry ingredients and mix until well blended. Roll into walnut-size balls. Flatten slightly on ungreased cookie sheet. Bake at 300 for 20 minutes or until golden brown. Cool on wire rack.

These cookies (originally called ANZAC biscuits in honor of the Australian New Zealand Army Corps) are great for sack lunches. They will keep fresh for a couple of weeks.

"Let us have some food set aside that would sustain us for a time in case of need. But let us not panic nor go to extremes. Let us be prudent in every respect."

President Gordon B. Hinckley
"The Times in Which We Live," Ensign, Nov. 2001, 72

141

FLAXSEED GINGERSNAPS

1 1/2 C. flaxseed meal
1/4 C. vegetable oil
1 C. granulated sugar
1/4 C. molasses
1 egg
1/2 C. water

2 C. wheat or white flour
2 tsp. baking soda
1/2 tsp. salt
1 tsp. ground cinnamon
2 tsp. ground ginger
1/4 tsp. cayenne pepper (opt.)

Cream first 6 ingredients in a large mixing bowl. In a separate bowl, sift dry ingredients together (if desired, add cayenne pepper to make ginger snaps a little hotter). Stir into creamed mixture. Drop by spoonfuls onto an ungreased cookie sheet lined with waxed paper. Bake at 375 for 10-12 minutes or until well-browned. Cool on wire rack.

PEANUT BUTTER GOODIES

1/2 C. butter, softened
1/2 C. peanut butter
1/4 C. honey
1/2 C. granulated sugar
1 egg

1 tsp. vanilla
2 C. whole-wheat flour
1/2 tsp. salt
1 tsp. baking soda
Sugar for dipping

Cream first 6 ingredients. Sift dry ingredients together. Stir into creamed mixture. Roll cookies into 1-inch balls. Roll in granulated sugar and place on ungreased cookie sheet. Press with fork tines. Bake at 350 for 10 minutes on top oven rack. Remove immediately. Cool on wire rack.

LEMON LOVE NOTES

Crust:
- 2 C. flour
- 1 C. butter
- 1/2 C. powdered sugar
- 1/2 tsp. salt

Filling:
- 2 C. sugar
- 4 Tbsp. dried eggs
- 1/2 C. lemon juice
- 1/2 C. flour
- 1/2 tsp. baking powder
- 1/2 tsp. salt

Mix the 4 crust ingredients together. Press into 9 x 13 baking pan. Bake at 350 for 15 minutes. Remove from oven. Meanwhile, whisk the 6 ingredients for the lemon filling together. Spread lemon filling over hot crust. Bake at 350 for 30 minutes.

Sprinkle with powdered sugar.

" LET US BE IN A POSITION SO WE ARE ABLE TO NOT ONLY FEED OURSELVES THROUGH THE HOME PRODUCTION AND STORAGE, BUT OTHERS AS WELL."

PRESIDENT EZRA TAFT BENSON, "PREPARE FOR THE DAYS OF TRIBULATION," ENSIGN, NOV. 1980, 33.

Have you ever noticed that whenever you start to think or talk about food storage, the subject of emergency preparedness always seems to come up? As already mentioned, food storage is not just for an emergency; it is meant to be used as part of our everyday life.

Actually, if you think about it, preparedness should be part of our everyday life as well. After all, we are always at risk of an emergency. Whether we are faced with a personal crisis where we are individually in need, or a community disaster where many people are affected, we should always be prepared.

There is so much information about this topic and not much space left in my book, so I am including a list in the back of this section of web sites that have information about emergency preparedness.

There are basically two kinds of crisis situations. We need to be prepared for both of them. This section has ideas and helps for both.

1. We are in our home and must remain there.

In this situation, we must survive on whatever we have in our home and rely on whatever plan we have established. Don't plan on anyone being able to help you. This may not be possible.

2. We are away from home or we must evacuate our home.

In this situation, we must survive on whatever we have with us or are able to take with us. It is likely that you would be in a hurry, so it is best to have items packed and ready to go.

I think the best advice while preparing for and handling an emergency comes from young Kevin in the movie Home Alone. *When he was faced with a huge crisis, he said to himself, "Don't get scared now!"*

EMERGENCY ESSENTIALS

Stay at Home

If a crisis situation demands that you stay at home, there are some things you need to know and do. Here's a list:

1. Have a plan for everyone who is away from home to get home.

> *Have you ever dreamed that you couldn't get to one of your children? I hate that dream! To me, this would be the biggest crisis of all. Make sure you have a plan!

> *Also, have a plan in case someone can't get home. What can he do?

2. Know and practice shut-off skills and emergency strategies.

> *Do you know where and how to shut off gas, water, and electricity? Do your children? Have you practiced doing it . . . lately? They can get tricky and sticky. Make sure all of you practice periodically.

> *Give everyone a specific assignment and practice it. It's helpful to rotate the assignments so everyone knows how to do everything.

3. Collect information and directions from local authorities.

> *Your city will have information about your area.
> *Make sure you have a battery-operated radio and fresh batteries.

4. Make sure you have sufficient food storage and supplies.

* What will you eat?

* Do you have adequate water stored?

5. Plan and purchase equipment to prepare for power outages.

* How will you keep warm?

* How will you cook?

* What will you use for lighting? Consider lanterns, fuel, candles, etc.

Evacuate Home

If a crisis situation demands that you evacuate your home, there are some things you need to know and do. Here's a list.

1. Prepare 72-hour kits for your family.

2. Create and practice a plan of evacuation.

3. Be informed about the different types of emergencies that could occur and their appropriate responses.

This list is adapted from the "Ready" campaign, U.S. Department of Homeland Security, whose goal is to educate and empower Americans to prepare and respond to potential emergencies. They said, "All Americans should have some basic supplies on hand in order to survive for at least three days if an emergency occurs." Their motto is, **"Prepare, Plan, Stay Informed."**

BASIC 72-HOUR KIT

* Water—One gallon per person per day—three-day supply
* Food (non-perishable)—At least a three-day supply
* Battery-powered or hand-crank radio and an NOAA Weather Radio with tone alert (include extra batteries for both)
* Flashlight and batteries (include extra batteries)
* First-aid kit
* Whistle to signal for help
* Dust mask to help filter contaminated air
* Plastic sheeting and duct tape to make shelter
* Moist towelettes, garbage bags, and plastic ties for personal sanitation
* Wrench or pliers to turn off utilities
* Can opener for food
* Local maps

These lists are from the "Ready" campaign, U.S. Department of Homeland Security

ADDITIONAL KIT ITEMS

* Prescription medications and glasses

* Infant formula and diapers

* Pet food and extra water for your pet

* Important family documents (such as copies of insurance policies, identification, and bank account records) in a waterproof, portable container

* Cash or traveler's checks and change

* Emergency reference material, such as first-aid book or information from www.ready.gov

* Sleeping bag or warm blanket for each person; consider additional bedding if you live in a cold-weather climate

* Complete change of clothing, including a long-sleeved shirt, long pants, and sturdy shoes; consider additional clothing if you live in a cold-weather climate

* Household chlorine bleach and medicine dropper (to use as a disinfectant, mix 9 parts water to 1 part bleach; to treat water, mix 16 drops bleach to 1 gallon water)

* Fire extinguisher

* Matches in waterproof container

* Feminine and personal hygiene supplies

* Mess kits, paper plates and cups, plastic utensils, paper towels

* Paper and pencil, books, games, and other activities for children

NON-PERISHABLE FOODS FOR 72-HOUR KITS

Food	Amount	Packaging
Cereal (dry)	2 cups	Zip-top bag
Crackers	8 ounces	Commercially packaged
Granola bars	3 1-oz. bars	Commercially packaged
Trail mix	8-12 ounces	Zip-top bag
Dried fruits	8-12 ounces	Zip-top bag
Milk	1 10-oz. can	Commercial cans
Milk (dry)	1 cup	Zip-top bag
Hot chocolate	4 envelopes	Commercially packaged
Fruit juice	18-36 ounces	Commercial box/pouch
Baby food	As per baby needs	Commercial jars/boxes
Tunafish	5-6 ounces	Commercial cans
Other meats	6 ounces	Commercial cans
Beans	8-16 ounces	Commercial cans
MREs	2-3 meals	Commercial pouches
Candy (hard)	3-4 ounces	Commercially wrapped
Candy bars	2-3 bars	Commercially wrapped

OTHER ACCESSORIES

Sewing kit
Rope/twine
Aluminum foil
Can opener

Safety pins
Shovel
Candles (survival)
Hand sanitizer

Fingernail clippers
Hammer/nails
Canned heat
Gloves

CONTAINERS

Five-gallon buckets with screw-top lids work very well for the main family kits (usually sold where food storage items are sold). You can pad and cover the lid to make a seat. It is nice to have one container with food and another bucket with tools, flashlight, and other supplies. For personal kits, a small backpack works best.

Prepare ye, prepare ye, for that which is to come . . .

D&C 1:12

BECAUSE IT'S ALWAYS BETTER TO "BEE" PREPARED!

72-HOUR KIT STORAGE

Emergency supplies should be stored in a place that is convenient for you to reach in a time of emergency. Personal kits could be stored in bedrooms. The family kit should be somewhere close to an outside entrance.

It is also wise to have an emergency kit in the trunk of your car. You might also want to store one at your workplace.

Food items should be rotated every six months. To help you remember to check bags, pick holidays that are opposite on the calendar, like Halloween and Easter, or opposite birthdays, like May and November.

Other 72-Hour Kit Items and Ideas

Other 72-Hour Kit Items and Ideas

INDEX